Carrying My Chalice

Carrying My Chalice

Oliver Powell

The Pilgrim Press
NEW YORK

Copyright © 1989 by The Pilgrim Press
All rights reserved

No part of this publication may be reproduced, stored in a retrieval system, or transmitted in any form or by any means, electronic, mechanical, photocopying, recording, or otherwise (brief quotations used in magazine or newspaper reviews excepted), without the prior permission of the publisher.

Permissions are incorporated in the Notes on pages 144–47.

Library of Congress Cataloging-in-Publication Data

Powell, Oliver.
  Carrying my chalice / Oliver Powell.
  ISBN 0-8298-0799-3
  1. Powell, Oliver. 2. United Church of Christ—Clergy—Biography. 3. United churches—United States—Clergy—Biography. I. Title.
BX9886.Z8P697   1989
285.8'34'0924—dc19
[B]   88-29988
                                                         CIP

The Pilgrim Press, 132 West 31 Street, New York, NY 10001

For Loey and Dave
who carry their chalices high
and with courage

The poet Yeats once spoke about the crucial importance for him of bearing safely the precious chalice of his own being.

CONTENTS

	Foreword	ix
CHAPTER 1	**The Leaf Mold of the Years**	1
CHAPTER 2	**Exodus**	10
CHAPTER 3	**The Surprises of Grace**	26
CHAPTER 4	**Wonders of the Journey**	51
CHAPTER 5	**Carrying My Chalice**	98
CHAPTER 6	**Loose Ends**	123
	Notes	144

FOREWORD

To deal with what remains—that is the assignment for these later, quieter, busy years. For there is a residue, a deposit of the days and decades that have gone before. There is the rubbish pile: shards of broken relationships, scraps of tinsel and lengths of faded ribbon from half-forgotten celebrations, handkerchiefs still moist with tears, sounds that will not altogether be silenced, scenes that still bruise the eye.

But as for Emily Dickinson, there is "my silver shelf," admitting no plated ware but only sterling kept polished against the tarnish of the years: the unquestioning trust of children and their pure laughter; the unconditional love of those closest to me, believing so much, bearing so much, even at the door of death; friends, yielding more happiness and security than they ever could have dreamed.

I have come to live comfortably with most of the residue. I can now walk past the rubbish heap with dignity. There are still unanswered questions there, but, as Rainer Maria Rilke said once, we are to live the questions, even those that will not, or cannot, be lived into fully satisfying answers.

And I celebrate the treasures with pure joy, though there are questions about them, too. The most stubborn has to do with accepting as my very own the holy mark of grace etched on each. But more and more, faith is having the last word, and little by little, the questions are being put to rest.

> Through many dangers, toils, and snares
> I have already come;
> 'Tis grace has brought me safe thus far,
> And grace will lead me home.[1]

This book is about that affirmation of faith.

CHAPTER 1

The Leaf Mold of the Years

> To care is to cherish because a thing is given, because every field of dishonor or of praise is alive in the rich leaf mold of the unfolding years.
> —Joseph Sittler

It came to me one day how many things in our home—on the walls, on tables, desks, and shelves—are there because of the people who have shared pieces of their lives with us. They are a fascinating collage of relationships and experiences that have given a distinctive shape and color to the years.

There are the photographs, each evoking its own response of joy, of pain, of pride: Loey and Dave at graduation time, and Joe, a few weeks before we walked with him up to the gates of death. There is Eleonore, nearing fifty, at *her* college commencement, twenty-six years after high school. There is Sue, ashine with her transparent grace; Kathryn, serenely poised in her special loveliness; and Jon in all the brightness of his spirit.

There are scenes of special importance: the gleaming ramparts of the Himalaya "snows"—Annapurna, Machapuchere, and the awesome massif of Kangchenjunga seen from the slopes of a Darjeeling tea plantation. There is the thunder of surf spending the furious backlash of an Atlantic hurricane on a rocky headland in Maine.

There are paintings, drawings, pieces of sculpture and pottery, lovingly crafted and given as a testimony to a particular relationship: Alice's bronze deer, of the forty-second psalm, gaunt and desperate in thirst, shaped on a bleak day in her life. Or Becky's soaring gull, her portrait of Andrew Wyeth, and her charcoal sketch of an Indian woman. There is Rob's woodcut of a modern troubadour, singing the merry, sad songs of people on America's underside. There are Sue's commentary in batik on our marriage; Allen's two rusty nails welded into a cross on a block of wood, "Thank" burned into its base; a banner spelling out in scarlet and shocking pink flames Moses' hair-raising experience in the wilderness—a gift from saints in a church I once served as an interim minister. There are also Anne's silhouette, "The Gardener," about me, she says, and my greenish thumb; poetry in flight in Joe's blue and silver Pegasus; Loey's photograph of the California redwoods and her searching expression in calligraphy, "Jesus, Grassroots Christ."

There is *High-over Farm,* by Elizabeth, who, at eighty, shifted her painting style from traditional representation to impressionism. And the Japanese prints, gift of a gracious lady who was a sturdy supporter and encourager in one of my ministries. There is Charles's collage, "Man: Bits and Pieces," fashioned of chopped-up playing cards, every king, queen, and jack of us blown about and dehumanized by the dusty swirls of contemporary living. Nearby is Eleonore's anniversary remembrance of Gerard Manley Hopkins's "Pied Beauty," done in stylized lettering. There are samples, too, of her elegant stitchery and of my own efforts in stained glass.

These are signs of a precious grace, bits and pieces themselves, of the sacrament of friendship and the sacredness of authentic relationships. They are visible evidence of priceless treasure stored in the spacious, echoing depository of my mind, a cassette of colorful experiences kept ready for instant replay: misty-eyed farewells, joyous homecomings, moments of ecstasy or of dark brooding. There are carnival days and merrymaking, coveted hours of solitude—surf watching, mountain hiking, or, tightly earphoned against intrusion, reliving with Renata Tebaldi, Desdemona's heartbreak in the last act of *Otello*. There is rejection; there is acceptance. There are tears and side-splitting laughter, pain and healing. There are moments of decision, loneliness, and, most treasured, the steadying hands and voices of those who know me, love me, and take me as I am—no questions asked.

It all has to do with the person I have turned out to be—lumps and liabilities, talents and treasures. As the years lengthen, my own "remembrance of things past" has taken on new dimensions. I have learned that there is far more than meets the eye or the ear in the quiet murmurings of memory. It is more than recalling people and experiences with affection and gratitude. In the end, it is a chronicle of the whole history of which I have been a part, the whole tradition out of which I have come. With exquisite awareness of the heart of a matter, Joseph Sittler says it this way in the *Ecology of Faith:* "To care is to cherish because a thing is given, because one has been there, because every field of dishonor or of praise is alive in the rich leaf mold of the unfolding years."

At any rate, it has been so with me and, I suspect, with us all and our yesterdays. Drifted and long since buried by the wind of seventy-six winters, the fallen leaves of all that I have known, enjoyed, suffered, and shared have not decomposed into a final forgetting. In the creative process of nature forever recycling its raw material, they have formed a rich, nourishing mold on the forest floor of my life. In Dag Hammarskjöld's words in *Markings*, it is like "a moist humus in the fertile darkness where the rain falls and the grain ripens—no matter how many tramp across the parade ground in whirling dust under an arid sky."

It is like what goes on in the compost pile at the bottom of the garden, dumping ground for weeds, grass, brush cuttings, and garbage. But, as a veteran gardener said once, compost is "the caviar of fertilizers." So, tending it scrupulously, turning it to the sun now and then, watering it, sprinkling it with limestone, the miracle is hastened. Bugs and microscopic organisms take over, transforming petals and potato peelings into a rich, crumbly compound to be dug into the soil to enable another harvest.

It is what makes the difference in the way I have learned to handle the past. In what Evelyn Underhill called "the great and secret economy of God," which conditions both our inner and our outer landscapes, I know that nothing is wasted or static. The old is forever reacting to the pressures of the new, change being the one changeless certainty. Pain has given way to healing and to the courage to bear it bravely. Grief has moved slowly toward quiet acceptance and a larger capacity to deal with death, when and however it comes. Failure has felt its way into sounder wisdom and set wider margins for error. Loss has led to astonishing discoveries of the truth about myself.

It all adds up to the importance of recognizing and celebrating the "given" in our lives. There are facts about me that I no longer feel it necessary to mask. There are things that can't be undone or done over. There are questions that will never be answered to my full satisfaction. There are betrayals of honor and decency that no longer need to torture my conscience. There are the moments when I was at my worst, and those when I simply did not do the best I could, in spite of the tendency to claim otherwise. But, there are, as well, the shining hours, glinting with sunlight and laughter, spilling over with unutterable, holy joy. There are the mornings broken "like the first morning," high noons of sheer delight, and the singular splendors of the night. It's all there, every "field of dishonor or of praise. . . . alive in the rich leaf mold of the unfolding years."

Sallie TeSelle says that, in the end, it is a matter of looking at one's life aesthetically. "An old man reviewing his life," she writes, is doing just that when he attempts to set aside the pattern it has assumed for him in order to see the exact curve of each twist and turn in it. His concentration on the particularity of each event . . . may result in a flash of insight that seems to be entirely new and yet, he would claim, is the true structure of the events. By diving beneath the conventions, he not only has discovered a new shape to his reality, but has also created this new shape, for apart from his insight, the order that emerges, although it is "in" the event, would have lain forever dormant.[1]

So far, so good. There is something to be said for "an old man reviewing his life," getting a new perspective on it, coming up with fresh insights. But, someone asks, isn't it essentially a private enterprise? What's so important about making it public? Moreover, isn't it presumptuous to assume that anyone else could possibly be interested? Celebrities can get away with it simply because of who they are. There is a healthy, or unhealthy, curiosity about their lives. But ordinary mortals are likely to consider their disclosures as unimportant, too commonplace for public scrutiny. Besides, there could be the accusation of exhibitionism and an unwarranted hankering for the spotlight. "How ridiculous, this need of yours to communicate!" wrote Hammarskjöld about sharing *his* inner journey. "Why should it mean so much to you that at least one person has seen the inside of your life?" Then, answering his own question, he proceeded to disclose all kinds of private experiences along his spiritual pilgrimage. The manuscript of *Markings* was discovered in his desk after his death with a letter addressed to a friend: "These entries provide the only true 'profile' that can be drawn," he wrote.

> That is why, during recent years, I have reckoned with the possibility of publication, though I have continued to write for myself, not for the public. . . . If you find them worth publishing, you have my permission to do so—as a sort of

white book concerning my negotiations with myself—and with God.[2]

I have come to believe that such documentation need not be restricted to saints, as priceless as their disclosures may be. In the foreword of his autobiography, Edmund Hilary said he discovered that even the mediocre can have adventures and that even the fearful person can achieve. To be sure, there is no substitute for the testimonies of the heroic and the saintly. Reading them, pondering their experiences on the summits will always be a source of spiritual power. But the chronicles of obscure travelers have a unique value. Much can be made of the modest reporting of novices and amateurs scrabbling on the lower slopes and, now and then, to their astonishment, stumbling upon a truth that stands their hair on end. We read of summit people with a kind of awesome reverence, blinded, perhaps intimidated, by such rarefied achievement. But we identify more readily with the less experienced, with their uncertain foothold, their groping, their slipping and sliding.

What I propose, then, in these pages is a kind of "white book," to sift through patches of the fertile leaf mold of the years, to examine briefly the curves of their twists and turns, hoping to discern more clearly the true shape of my being. For this present moment, before darkness begins to thicken, is a time of gathering, of summing up, of disclosing and honoring whatever pattern the vagrant years have traced.

It is in the way Josephine Johnson put it in her heartbreaking novel, *Now in November*. It was Eleonore's gift to me on my twenty-fifth birthday. We read it together. Its sombre beauty, its unsparing exploration of interior landscapes moved us profoundly. Strange, in a way, that it should, given the mood we were in in those blithe days, when everything was yeast, high spirits, and hope. But looking back, I can see that the tale was more about me than either of us could suspect. Now, after fifty years, the novel's first sentences have come full circle.

> Now in November, I can see our years as a whole. The autumn is like both an end and a beginning to our lives, and those days which seemed confused with the blur of all things too near and too familiar are clear now. . . . I can look back and see the days as one looking down on things past, and they have more shape and meaning than before.[3]

This business of sharing private treasure may not be as important as I make it out to be. But as Loren Eiseley has put it, "that the self and its minute adventures may be interesting, every essayist from Montaigne to Emerson has intimated." Certainly, in a time like this when ideas and convictions are so easily molded by the pressure of mass opinion and manipulated into orthodoxy by the media of mass communication, personal, face-to-face testimony becomes especially urgent. John Donne said once that as his life went on, he developed less and less interest about the truth in general and more desperation about the truth for himself.

Moreover, in these later years, all of this has taken on an urgent faith dimension. That is to say, I find myself asking more and more often: Exactly how much of the good news of the love and grace of God do I own simply because it is about me? How much have I, myself, experienced of the new life in Christ? Can I speak authoritatively of the New Being, of forgiveness, and of a fresh start because I know what it is to face bankruptcy and the awesomeness of having to begin again?

Actually, the good news of the love of God made plain in the life, death, and victory over death of Jesus Christ is either about me in an intense personal way, or it isn't about anybody. In John Macquarrie's words in *Thinking About God*, truth always has a personal dimension. "Truths," he said, "do not float around the universe like clouds of cosmic dust. Truths are truth for *someone*. They are not so much properties as events."

The apostle Paul made the most convincing case for it. New life is the heart of the Christian message, and, like him, I confess to know a lot about it. My life can be described quite accurately as a form of rescue operation. Firsthand, I know what it means to be lost and what it means to be found, not in the ecstasy of an altar call but in far more searching and hard-nosed ways. Many truths have become events for me because of movements in my life of a power quite beyond my managing and certainly beyond my deserving.

There is a risk that I know only too well: Theology put in autobiographical form implies vulnerability. It means having to let your pain show, allowing people who are desolate to know that you have crouched in the same cold and dark, anxiously waiting for it to be light again. It means realizing, probably to your surprise, that spiritual reality may be discovered more often in the wintry seasons of the heart than in the summery ones. It means listening to a "cry of absence" as well as to the voice of a comforting, consoling presence, as Martin Marty has eloquently put it.

But when we share both the defeats and the victories on our personal battlefronts, we are doing more theologizing than we suspect. Thoreau once shared a piece of his salted-down wisdom on this score. He told about an unhappy experience he once had with a certain minister. In fact, he said, he was tempted to stop going to church. The minister's sermons gave no intimation that the man ever laughed or wept, that he was married or in love, that he had been commended or chagrined. He had not learned the main secret of the preacher's profession, namely, to convert life into truth. After all, said Thoreau, the true preacher can best be known by the way he or she deals out to people his or her life—life passed through the fire!

Here, then, is a "white book" concerning my negotiations with myself and with God. Burnished by pain and at times a fierce loneliness, glinting with bits and pieces of heady joy, supported by the love of family and friends so sturdy that it brings the tears, and beyond all, buttressed by the prodigal caring of a God who has never let me go, I make public things that have been largely private. I do so with some words of Emerson in mind. Daughter Loey once inscribed them for me on a homemade birthday card: "The only gift is a portion of thyself."

Chapter 2

Exodus

> "The Lord brought us out of Egypt with a mighty hand."
> —Deuteronomy 6:21

There are pieces of Egypt still in me, and I know that I shall never get them all out. Nonetheless, the theme of my tale is liberation, a long, often darkened journey from bondage to the freedom of self-ownership. Looking back on it now, I can see it as a whole. I can understand essentially what happened: I acknowledged my captivity. I recognized that circumstances I took for granted actually were crippling limitations, and that as long as I continued to huddle in the shelter of a safe, stifling environment, I could not be in touch with the authentic person I was meant to be. Beyond that, what took place had all the marks of a rescue operation.

It came off as well as it did largely because my rescuers knew their business and because they had a heavy investment of love in me. Putting it in religious language it signifies unmistakable evidence of the grace of God at work.

Having to look at the truth about myself and coming to terms with it was the heart of the matter. There is a parallel and a parable in Eugene O'Neill's play *The Iceman Cometh*. It is a long and verbose exploration of a familiar human plight: stitching together a set of illusions about yourself and then one frightening day being pressured to examine them and to face the unembroidered truth.

The scene is the bar of Harry Hope's (!) sleazy, last-chance hotel on New York's West Side. The characters are a grubby collection of men at the brink of oblivion, hanging on by their fingernails. There is a one-time Harvard law student, a one-time editor—all of them "one-time." Each lives behind his own barricade of illusion erected against reality, against the person he might have been, against the one indispensable element that makes one a bona fide human being.

One day, an old, trusted friend they haven't seen for years shows up—Hickey, a hardware salesman. He tells them that he has had a shattering, life-changing experience and that because of it, he has a message of salvation for them. He's there, he says, to save them, not from booze but from their pipe dreams.

> I know now from my experience that they're the things that really poison and ruin a guy's life, and keep him from finding any peace. If you knew how free and contented I feel now! I'm like a new man. . . . And the cure. . . . It is so damned simple once you have the nerve. Just the old dope of honesty is the best policy—honesty with yourself I mean. Just stop lying about yourself and kidding yourself about your tomorrows. . . . Oh, I know how you resent the way I have to show you up. I don't blame you. I know from my own experience it's bitter medicine, facing yourself in the mirror with the old false whiskers off. But. . . . I swear. . . . it will be worth it to you in the end, after you're rid of lying to yourselves about you're something you're not.[1]

But Hickey's efforts are wasted. Each man stirs briefly to make a feeble response, but the odds of reality are too great. Having the props knocked out from under them is more than they can handle, and one by one they fall back into drowsy despair.

You might say about Hickey, as some commentators have, that he is a literary device, a Christ figure, coming to break open a situation and to offer a solution. To be sure, he is anything but a Christ-like person, but we have to admit that frequently people and situations that cannot be so described are conveyers of the truth, as well as the saints!

This, of course, was the trouble the Jews in Jesus' day had with him. Were they to use that term, in their eyes there was nothing "Christ-like" about him. Nor were they in a mood to take any lip from a free-swinging, rabble-rousing young rabbi with no credentials. He turned to them one day and said: "Look, if somehow you can get inside what I'm talking about, you shall know the truth, and the truth will set you free." But they hadn't the slightest idea of what he was talking about!

God knows it took me long enough to get inside of it! I heard it in my head often enough through years of sermons and study sessions, but never, really, in the caves and crevices of my spiritual insides where, in the end, such things have to be listened to and heard. But there came the day when a window opened on a long-closed, stuffy room. I felt the stirring of fresh air and heard new sounds. I can talk about it now in a way that sounds academic. At the time, however, it wasn't anything like that. It never is when an old mold begins to shatter and you haven't any idea what shape the raw stuff of your life is going to take. There was a lot of pain and darkness. That was disconcerting because Christians, I had been taught, were supposed to be upbeat and cheery.

At any rate, something new and intimidating was beginning to filter through the murk. It was a growing awareness that there were truths about me that needed to be claimed, that I needed to make an ampler, braver response to life.

The saving, turnabout truth in my life is that by grace I was able to make a new response. It couldn't have happened without the pressure and encouragement of people who loved me, or without my being able to scrape together all the meager store of courage I could get my hands on in order to face myself "in the mirror with the old false whiskers off," as Hickey put it. It's important for me now to put what was happening in theological terms, in the language of faith, and this "mirror" metaphor was the start of it. Pushed and nudged by others, one way or another, I managed the first faltering and frightening steps toward self-honesty. I often think how professional counseling could have helped me at this point. But those were years when therapy was uncommon, a highly experimental, expensive, and questionable option and, for the most part, unavailable to people like me. To give myself credit, I stuck with the rugged, distasteful, and lonely business of self-scrutiny, all the time sensing the support of the friends who stood by, most of whom were anchored in the realities of the Christian faith, believing that there is, indeed, a love that bears all things, believes all things, hopes all things, endures all things. I realize now how much I depended upon them for support and encouragement as we met one another, cared for one another, were ruthlessly honest with one another. The group we were part of provided a kind of "mirror" opportunity for self-growth, and we came to be dependent on, and grateful for, it. If Martin Luther was right in saying that we are to be "little Christs" to one another, I can understand what is meant by the saying that Christ himself is a mirror for each of us. We look into his compassionate face, and after a while, a quiet flow of knowledge sets in. We are given data about ourselves we have never been able to accept or even think about. We are offered an invitation to explore potential we never entertained as possibility.

As the months went by, I moved closer to the raw truth at the heart of the gospel, the good news about everybody's life: You are loved! You are loved unconditionally by other people. You are loved in the same way by God who never gives up on you in spite of any discrediting views you hold of yourself or of a temptation to abandon yourself as a lost cause. When I could own that elemental truth, I could say that I was on the way to freedom.

It snapped into focus in a wild dream I had one night. I

can recall it as vividly as when I awoke from it. It is true, as a character in Edward Albee's *A Delicate Balance* puts it, that "we sleep to let the demons out!"

It was the blackest of nights. I was alone beneath the grape arbor that sheltered the kitchen door of my childhood home—where much was right, but more was wrong. I heard an ominous rumble of thunder in the heavy, windless air and felt a curdling sense of foreboding, as of something immensely evil and shattering about to happen. The terror in me mounted and pushed the dream to nightmare pitch. I was aware of a growing anger in me, against what or whom I could not say. Unable to contain myself longer, I ran out from under the arbor and threw myself down beside the flower bed, which, as a child, I cultivated each summer. There next to the unsuspecting zinnias and marigolds, I shouted in rage into the blackness of the night. Suddenly there was an awesome stillness and my panic slowly drained away. I looked down the long stretch of garden to the borderline of trees at the far end, now standing in sharp outline as flashes of a rosy, beneficent light pierced the darkness. Then I saw an animal standing quite still—a horse, a doe, I couldn't tell. The light faded and for a moment I was caught up in the old terror. But when I lifted my head, a surge of inexpressible relief washed over me. Great bolts of clouds were being swept away by an eastward-fleeing wind, like curtains being drawn apart, disclosing the night sky jeweled with galaxies of glittering stars. I came wide awake with a smile and a warm sense of well-being.

A brief sketch of my growing-up years will help to make clear what was going on.

It would take years of therapy, I'm sure, to unravel the tangled threads that held us together as a family but also snared us, there in that red-shingled house in Queens. It was where the basic pattern for my days was drawn. There we enjoyed, helped, misunderstood, and mistreated one another, and when things became unmanageable, it was from there that I escaped.

To all appearances, we were a typical middle-class household in the first quarter of the century. A Puritan hand was laid heavily upon us: We were Presbyterians, church oriented and strictly Calvinist in our morality. There was a no-nonsense Sabbath observance—two services of worship and a ban on movie going and other "worldly" entertainments. Card playing, except for the "old maid" variety, was suspect. Wine and spirits were not only outlawed, they were the unmistakable marks of immorality.

Curiously, it was in the shadow of this particular prohibition that I found occasion for my first instance of public protest. It came about with the annual visit of a temperance worker to the Junior Department of our Sunday School. At the conclusion of her emotionally charged presentation, she distributed pledge cards, which we were asked to sign and return the following Sunday. In the pledge, we were to forswear the consumption of all alcoholic beverages for the rest of our lives—beer, wine, hard liquor, and, to my astonishment, cider. I was not terribly well informed on the subject, but I was not persuaded that cider, certainly not the kind we had at Thanksgiving dinner, came under an official ban. After a brief struggle, I signed and returned the card but scratched out "cider," wondering if there would be a kickback. There was none.

Our Puritan orientation allowed that human sexuality existed, but it certainly was not a subject for discussion or analysis. Consequently, my understanding of my sexual nature was abysmally limited, and most of what I did know was picked up in remarks or conversations or surreptitiously scrounged from any likely source of information.

For all the seeming normality about us as a family, there were essentially unhealthy configurations in our relationship, and, in the long run, they proved to be our undoing. We had only the best of intentions toward one another, but without our ever really understanding what was going on, the psychic baggage each of us carried proved to be too heavy. Family loyalty and solidarity, which I had taken for granted, gradually crumbled and for me, ended up in hostility and alienation. That was the bitterest part, and when, finally, the family read me out of their circle, I was bewildered and hurt. But the focus on it all has shifted. Now I am able to peer back along the misty corridors of the years and, "like the world seen through a tear," to borrow Loren Eiseley's phrase, remember my family without bitterness. The resentment I felt against them for a long time has been defused, and I can honor them for who they were, or tried to be.

On a recent visit to New York, I walked around the old neighborhood. It was depressing to see that it had become an ugly slum. The old family house was gone, burned to the ground, I learned. The house next door, which had been a speakeasy during Prohibition days, and whose mysterious, nocturnal comings and goings we avidly monitored from our upstairs windows, was a dilapidated, fourth-class rooming house. The rest of the block was a squalid clutter—an abandoned gas station, a tavern, a row of boarded-up houses. I walked past the school I attended, where among my learnings was what it means to be part of a racial minority, the school at the time being 80 percent black. It was still there, a graffiti-blighted survivor in a cultural wilderness.

The scene struck me as a metaphor for the way our family life caved in, unable to survive the strains put upon it. With the sharpness of hindsight, I have recognized what was missing in our life together: We were lacking what it takes to survive. We were a terminal rather then a launching area, a place to come back to rather than start out from. Five of the seven of us had done just that—come back home after an encounter with death. First, my mother, following my father's death in the typhoid epidemic of 1912, with my half brother and with me, at three months, a survivor of spinal meningitis, by a narrow squeak. Five years later, we were joined by my mother's brother and his small daughter. His wife and son were both victims of the influenza epidemic of 1917. Another member of the household was a bachelor, my mother's youngest brother. Presiding over us all was the matriarch, my grandmother, doing the best she could to hold together an unstable emotional mix. She was a wise, essentially buoyant woman. She did what she could to deal with the heavy freight of needs and feelings, which she never quite understood, especially those of my mother, who was showing signs of not being able to cope. In our Wasp culture, it was assumed that situations indicating mental or emotional disorder were simply to be endured. It was one of the requirements of Puritan discipline. But should conditions become really serious, a person would, of course, have to be "put away." As I walked home from church with my grandmother one Sunday, she told me that that was exactly what would have to be done with my mother unless things got better. I have not forgotten the sense of terror that gripped me.

I do not have clinical evidence for it, but I know that my mother was shadowed by an undefined neurosis. Something was not "right," as we would say. The only attention I can recall being paid to her condition were vague references by relatives to her as "nervous," meaning that allowances had to be made. The unhealthiest sign of disability was a steadily growing fixation upon me, as though I were becoming the center of her world. She became jealous and resentful of time I spent with others away from home. Once, coming home from a friend's house later than expected, I found her in hysterics and the house in an uproar. There was the time when I was invited to join a group of younger people for a vacation trip. It was to be my first trip away from home. But she staged such a distressing scene of protest that the family gave in to her pleading and the idea was scotched.

The situation steadily worsened, but it wasn't until I had finished college that the problem began to come light. I go back repeatedly to a scene in Tennessee Williams's play, *The Night of the Iguana*. It's a parable of sorts of what was going on in my life at the time. Shannon, a priest whose life has come apart, and Hannah, who has never quite got hers together, are comparing notes. He asks her how she ever got through the things she had to face. "I was lucky," she says. "My work, this occupational therapy I gave myself—painting and doing quick character sketches—made me look out of myself, not *in*, and gradually, at the far end of the tunnel I was struggling out of, I began to see this very faint gray light, and kept climbing toward it. I had to." "Did it stay a gray light?" Shannon asks. "No," she replies, "it turned white." "Only white, never gold?" he pursues. "No, it stayed only white, but white is a very good light to see at the end of a long black tunnel you thought would never be ending, that only God or death could put a stop to."[2]

As a former tunnel dweller, my testimony is that by the grace of God somehow we keep climbing; patches of gray do turn to white and, now and then, to gold! But not without struggle and pain, and surely not without the gracious intervention of a few people who let it be known that their caring is unqualified and their love unconditional.

I celebrate three rescuers. First, there was Aunt Carrie. She was a great aunt, a public school teacher in the East Bronx, in one of the "blackboard jungles" of New York. Her job took courage and the kind of tough forthrightness with which she approached me one day. She admitted to me that she had kept an eye on the games we played in our household and thought it was time I got out on my own. Since I was about to begin college, she said I could have a room in her apartment, close to the campus of New York University.

Her investment in me was an important part of my exodus journey. Not only was I free of the suffocating climate of the family, but doors began to open all over the place! My aunt was a avid theatergoer, music lover, and traveler. She frequently invited me to join her on her excursions, especially into New York's world of the arts. Through it all, gently but firmly, and with the same no-nonsense directness by which she managed the roughnecks in her classroom, she encouraged me to take risks I would not have contemplated on my own. In short, she was one of the first people I had known to help me celebrate and enjoy the fact that I was meant to be a unique person, one Oliver Powell, and not a faded carbon copy of someone else.

My second rescuer was a feisty, opinionated, but at the core truly caring woman, who before too long, was to become my mother-in-law. I had finished college by the time I met her, and was in a vocational vacuum. The Great Depression of the thirties had wiped out the possibility of any openings for the teaching job (Romance languages) for which I was accredited, and I had settled for a mindless clerical job at twelve dollars a week. I had gone back to live with "the family," knowing that, in a way, I was backsliding but not seeing an alternative. I still had things to learn about being on my own. I was in an emotional slump, feeling genuinely sorry for myself.

My grandmother, now full of years and a great weariness, became terminally ill. A nurse was engaged to care for her during the day, the rest of us taking turns during the night. One of my responsibilities was to drive the nurse home after her tour of duty. We became well acquainted and good friends. Her own coping with a wretched marriage and a household forever teetering on the brink of financial disaster made her, I am sure, especially sensitive to signs of unhappiness in others. She spotted them in me. Her instincts put her squarely on target, and like Aunt Carrie, being geared for action, she told me in no uncertain terms that what I needed to do was to get away from my smothering environment. She invited me to live in her home. So, for the second time round, to the family's dismay and my mother's ill-disguised hurt, I packed my belongings and left.

At the center of this ferment was her daughter, Eleonore, my third and chief rescuer. Little by little we came to know each other, need each other, love each other. Looking back on the experience, we can see that in our mutual acceptance we were carrying out a mutual rescue operation. We were both wilderness people, aliens from families that could not acknowledge who we were and did not know quite what to do with us. I have described my home life; hers was even more beleaguered: a children's home for a number of years, or joyless, temporary quarters staked out at the edge of poverty.

Our lives drew steadily closer. We held on to each other in the fast-ebbing tide of family support. We made important decisions. We tackled the matter of my vocation. One day, for the first time, we talked about seminary and the ministry. Nobody had ever before suggested the possibility. I gulped inconclusively, but others joined her encouragement. I applied, and was accepted, as a student at Union Theological Seminary in New York.

The announcement of our engagement dropped with a leaden thud in the circle of my family. I tried to draw my mother into the circle of love for Eleonore, but it was more than she could handle. I suspect that any prospective daughter-in-law would have met with the same civilly marked rejection. When occasions brought us together, there were no "incidents," because in our household nothing was ever allowed to ruffle the mantle of decorum draped over us all, but the air was chilly and conversation eggshell fragile.

The families came to the wedding, on their best behavior. It was a long, moon-walk step on the exodus journey—that recessional down the aisle, that flight over the church steps and across the border into the Promised Land! There was a sense of finality about it but much more of a beginning. As a character in one of Tom Stoppard's plays says, "Every exit is an entrance somewhere else."

A final break with the family came when a decision had to be made about my mother's care. I was the one to make it. She had been living quite happily in a modest retirement home, following my grandmother's death and the breakup of the old household. But a form of progressive arteriosclerosis took over, and the retirement home informed me that they could no longer take responsibility for her. As I expected, the family had one solution: She would come and live with Eleonore and me. (We were now in our first parsonage.) It was, of course, wholly out of the question, if for no other reason than that we could not provide the custodial care she needed. The only solution was to commit her to a state institution. My decision to do so was the proverbial last straw for family relationships. Brother, aunts, uncles—all let me know what they thought of me. I was swamped by an outpouring of anger and rejection: To think that a son—and a Christian minister, at that—could so treat his mother! I made a number of efforts to bring about a reconciliation but with no results. We met briefly on the occasion of my mother's funeral in the atmosphere of icy, barely concealed animosity.

It ended there. My relatives went their way: I went mine. Were there not other things I could have done? Probably. Whether there were or not, I have long since shucked a sense of guilt, which, in pure Puritan style, tried to attach itself to me. If there is to be some further, ultimate accounting for my behavior, I know that it will be handled by a wisdom wiser than my own or than that of those who passed judgment on me.

Along with the risk taking, the wounding and scarring, the closing and opening of doors, the blunders and the backsliding, a new life was coming into being. It's what Eddie Anderson had to say about himself. Eddie is the hero, or nonhero, of Elia Kazan's novel *The Arrangement*. It can hardly be called a great novel, but it is an uncannily perceptive case study of new life being born out of the old.

It is about a man at the pinnacle of success in the advertising business. Through a series of experiences and under the scrutiny of an innate honesty, he comes to realize that practically everything about his life is phony. He courageously admits it, and the novel becomes a shattering search for his true identity. He peels off layer after layer of pretense until everything he had depended on for security is gone, and he is reduced to a cipher. One day, at the bottom of his despair, it becomes plain to him what is happening. "I understood clearly," he says,

> what it was I'd been feeling. . . . simply that I was two people. One was Eddie who behaved in predictable ways, concealed his animosities beneath a smile, and snuffed out his resentments before they got too hot. Then there was another man. He had no name yet, no face. But he was aborning as sure as Eddie was dying. These two people were locked in a deadly struggle, one slowly conquering the other. When the time came, Eddie would die and whoever was replacing him would be me. As soon as that death happened, the franchise would go to a new incumbent. A person, no less than a business has a right to go bankrupt, pay some debt, or perhaps a small percentage on all, and then start again. The emergent should not have to carry through the rest of his life the full weight of obligations to the mistakes and missteps Eddie had made.[3]

It is not exactly scripture, but is has a New Testament ring to it. My story is different from Eddie's in many ways, but he and I are blood brothers. We both took the risk of making a claim on the promise of new life, and we both cashed in—by hook or by crook, Eddie might say, but for me, by the grace of God. We escaped from bondage to freedom the hard way. Scarred by the struggle and discouraged now and then by setbacks, nonetheless, I own Dag Hammarskjöld's wisdom that "life pursues her experiments beyond the limitations of our own judgment." That truth still holds me steady. But there is an even greater one. It is to say that in my case, the pursuer, the "rescuer," was the love of God, the heavenly hound, nipping at my heels, nagging at my indolence until I was ready to risk an exodus journey and seek the freedom I needed in order to be an authentic human being.

Slowly, sometimes painfully, I learned what it means to be liberated and to practice it. For one thing, I began to claim the freedom of self-ownership against the bondage of conformity. Things like that never happen overnight, and, like the Children of Israel, I still have moments of longing to be back in Egypt, and act accordingly. Saying it another way, it's the business of staying in charge of your own life, knowing, accepting, and liking who you are, and not allowing people or situations to violate whatever that implies. As Robert Bolt said of Sir Thomas More, the hero of his play *A Man for All Seasons,* he was a man with "an adamantine sense of his own self. He knew where he began and where he left off, what area of himself he could yield to the encroachments of his enemies and what to the encroachments of those he loved."

"Egypt" means, of course, different things to different people. It may be family, the neighborhood, the crowd you keep company with, fellow workers, the administration in Washington or at Town Hall. In any one of these situations, there are accommodations that can be made, practicing the fine art of honorable compromise. But, I discovered, the moments of testing come when the demand for conformity to traditional standards and conventions violates what is an essential part of me as an authentic person. It means keeping unremitting vigilance over what I recognize as the inner core of my integrity.

Staying in charge! I'll always remember how once I was rudely brought up short on the urgency of that. I was attending a human relations laboratory where a group of us, under sensitive professional leadership for two weeks, scoured one another's lives. I was bruised at the end of the sessions, but I emerged a healthier human being. One day, during the discussion, I suddenly heard the leader talking to *me.* In his blunt, salty style, he said, "Look, for the life of me, I can't figure out who is in charge of you at this moment. I'm sure it's not you. I think it's somebody you've allowed to take over, somebody who has no right to do so. You can't allow that. Now, take a minute to find out who it is, look him straight in the eye, and fire the bastard!"

I discovered that liberation adds a new dimension to

living. Once delivered from things that keep you in bondage, you quit deciding and managing things "by the book," so to speak, and come to trust a way of getting at things that is free flowing and never wholly predictable. It's what is meant by the French word *élan*, which is strictly not translatable; "spirit" comes close: a flaming up, an inner burning and buoyancy.

In *The Guns of August,* Barbara Tuchman says that it was élan that accounted for the success of the French armies at the Battle of the Marne. It bewildered and frustrated the Germans, who fought according to the books. "French élan," wrote one of their generals, "just when it is on the point of being extinguished, flames up powerfully." Or, as another officer said,

> "The basic reason for German failure at the Marne was the extraordinary and peculiar aptitude of the French soldier to recover quickly. That men will let themselves be killed where they stand, that is a well-known thing and counted on in every plan of battle. But that men who have retreated for days, sleeping on the ground and half-dead with fatigue, should be able to take up their rifles and attack when the bugles sound, is a thing upon which we never counted. It was a possibility not studied in our war academy."[4]

Coming to terms with the truth about myself required élan. So did practicing the new kind of behavior that goes with it. For old patterns of behavior, things I learned in the "academy," stubbornly intrude, and like the Children of Israel in the wilderness, I fall back on them now and then. It's then I realize that it was only by a very narrow margin that I got out of Egypt at all!

But I *did* get out! And occasionally I indulge in some uninhibited celebration. There is a lot to be said for Yul Brynner's response to being given a special citation by the

New York theater Tony awards upon winding up more than four thousand performances of *The King and I*. After a few conventional words of gratitude spoken on such occasions, he added: "And thanks to Yul Brynner, who turned out not so badly after all!"

CHAPTER 3

The Surprises of Grace

> When grace doesn't come from the right, it comes from the left. When it doesn't come straight, it comes bent, and when it doesn't come bent, it comes broken. When it doesn't come from above, it comes from below; and when it doesn't come from the center, it comes from the circumference.
> —Charles Péguy

It is when I am trying hardest to unscramble a situation that won't come straight or that doesn't make sense that I become especially aware of a towering fact about my life: that my days are overshadowed and illumined by mysteries that are largely unexplainable.

The British scientist Bernard Lovell goes to the heart of the matter in saying that while scientific research of observable phenomena is an essential occupation of modern society, it does not embrace the totality of human purpose. We may, for example, send a space probe to the planet Venus, but we may never apprehend the ethos of the evening star.

For me, that stakes out the claims of faith more eloquently and persuasively than most scholarly treatises. Behind all the phenomena of the natural world and the data of human experience, there is a vast mystery to be probed, never to be fully apprehended. Time and again we creep up to the edges of it but are stopped in our tracks. Take, for example, the sunset to end all sunsets a few years back that flared over eastern Massachusetts one October day. It lifted thousands of dulled eyes skyward, snarled traffic, and made the headlines on the six o'clock news. It was a special dispatch from another realm delivered to a tired world winding down at the end of another routine day.

Or it may be the moment of death when someone you have loved beyond any telling of it slips over the horizon of everything you've been sure about, when the heart breaks into a thousand pieces, as ours did when our seventeen-year-old son Jonathan died. Or the ecstasy of such unexpected good news that the sleeping lark in me wakens and "soars up and up for very joy!"

It's for certain that whether we are awestruck, humbled, or exalted, soon or late, in one way or another, we brush against the mystery. Walter Bagehot once put it this way. "We live on the very edge of two dissimilar worlds; on the very line on which the infinite, unfathomable sea surges up, and just where the queer little bay of this world ends. We count the pebbles on the shore and imagine to ourselves, as best we may, the secrets of the great deep." An African tribesman, describing the religion of his people to a Westerner, said it in more primitive terms. "We hear something go by in the tops of the trees at night, but we do not speak of it."

People of faith *do* speak of it, of course. We try to count the pebbles a little more accurately than others, to pay special attention to the whispering in the treetops, and, as accurately as we can, report what we hear. But, after a time, the most perceptive among us stammer into silence, disappointed and frustrated. We'd so much like to have crystal-clear answers to our big questions, and we tend to cluster around those who claim to give them. In so doing, however, we are likely to end up like Nicodemus, there in the gospel record. More than anything, he wanted Jesus to clear up once and for all some nagging mysteries that clouded his thinking. And what came of that famous midnight conversation was simply more mystery and confusion. In the manner of the African tribesman, Jesus referred him, of all things, to the wind! It "blows wherever it wishes," he said. "You hear the sound it makes, but you do not know where it comes from or where it is going." Or take the woman who was caught red-handed in the act of adultery. No mystery there, people said, and the law and tradition were quite explicit on how to handle the situation. But, says the record, Jesus bent over and began to doodle in the sand!

The Bible is pervaded by mystery from beginning to end, as are the assumptions on which our Christian faith is based; there are so many things for which there is no strict accounting. You ask the question, "What does it all mean?" and you learn that mystery itself is part of the answer. I have been able to put down the roots of that truth into my hard-won experience at various points. For instance, I realize that in what I have referred to as my "escape from Egypt," the mystery of the grace of God was at work. Surely it was evident in the efforts of those "rescuers" and others who made a personal investment in that particular exercise in liberation.

There are other instances, equally telling. There were the dark days when I touched bottom in the long, frustrating, and finally abandoned search to find a job opportunity in my chosen profession—teaching Spanish and French to high school students. I had a feel for teaching, enjoyed it, and, based on limited experience, was fairly good at it. And I had the necessary academic accreditation: years of language study in high school and college, plus the required educational and "method" courses. The difficulty was elemental: There simply were no jobs. By the mid-thirties, schools everywhere were feeling the weight of the Great Depression. Budgets were cut to the bone, and if any opening appeared, it was certain to be filled by an experienced teacher who had been laid off earlier.

One cold, rainy January day, I took the bus from New York to Asbury Park, New Jersey, for the only job interview I had been offered in two years. It went badly. I sensed that the interviewing committee had little intention of hiring an inexperienced candidate when there was such a large supply of veteran teachers waiting to be called back. I was politely thanked for coming, and that, I knew, was that! With time on my hands before the bus trip home, I walked along the Asbury Park pier. The rain had stopped, but a bitter, wet wind raked the empty beach. It happened to be a few weeks after the *Morro Castle* disaster. The liner had caught fire and in order to save as many lives as possible, the captain had beached it. There it was in the gathering darkness, several hundred yards offshore, a fast ebbing tide sucking past its blackened hulk. A wave of self-pity engulfed me. Melodramatically I pictured the ship as the symbol of a blighted career. I walked to the bus depot in mourning, certain of a dream not deferred but obliterated.

But then the surprise: light after the dark—a sudden shift from teaching to ministry. Up to that time, I had never entertained the ministry as an option, nor had anyone else who knew me, for that matter. But it soon became all I could think about. Urged on by a few close friends, especially Eleonore, I applied for admission at two seminaries, was accepted at both, and settled for Union Theological in New York. There was an enthusiasm about it which I realized I had never felt for teaching. Looking back, I recognize how much thoughtful, caring friends had to do with it, but I honestly believe that I was yielding to the steady pressure of the Beyond laid against an important piece of my life.

Again, and more recently, another resolution, another coming to terms with the world I am meant to inhabit. Coming to Pilgrim Place in California, a retirement community for religious workers, I brought with me most of the professional luggage I had used during the years of active ministry: a commanding sense of responsibility and duty linked to a sizable capacity for hard work, to the point, at times, of compulsion. Retirement as a legitimate opportunity for letting go, for relishing a more leisurely pace, for the sheer enjoyment of interests and activities uniquely my own (and for which I mistakenly believed I had never had the time)—most of this escaped me. In short, retirement, in my reading of it, was simply a new locale for a continuum of busyness and disciplined commitment.

I have recently been overhauling that concept, to the discomfort of my monitoring Puritan. Again, grace, mysterious grace at work. It has come to me through the gentle pressure of a dear friend who cares deeply about me and who has watched my "workaholism" over the years. His own relaxed, laid-back style and his gentle chiding have proved to be an effective remedy in treating an illness that has afflicted more than one minister of the church. I've a way to go yet, but I am learning how to live more comfortably with unscheduled stretches of time, to give priority to things that delight and nourish me. As my son Dave said in a recent letter, "Take some of Ed's advice and try a small dose of guilt-free retirement."

For all our sophisticated technology and our expertise, like the weather and the changing seasons, the grace of God is beyond human management. It is like the rushing of the wind in the treetops; we hear the sound it makes, but we do not know where it is coming from or where it is going. And it is full of astonishing surprises. "When grace doesn't come from the right," says Charles Péguy,

> it comes from the left. When it doesn't come straight, it comes bent, and when it doesn't come bent, it comes broken. When it doesn't come from above, it comes from below; and when it doesn't come from the center, it comes from the circumference.[1]

This Beyond in our midst, as it has been called, is the assurance I have that for all my self-centeredness, my indolence, my shabby betrayals of the truth, a Spirit, a Presence incessantly broods over me never willing to let me out of its sight or to give up on me.

Grace comes into our lives in various guises. Have a look now at some of the particular, often strange, ways it has moved into mine.

A View From the Underside

"When grace doesn't come straight, it comes bent, and when it doesn't come bent, it comes broken. When it doesn't come from above, it comes from below."

I learned recently of an elderly alumnus of a certain Midwest college who at commencement time attended the seventieth reunion of his class. He was appropriately honored at a banquet, and in the course of his response he had this to say. "In all my years, if there is one thing I have learned more important than any other, it is to recognize the truth when I hear it, no matter how unpalatable or from however unlikely a source."

It was fairly late in my life and career as a minister before I came to appreciate that prickly slice of wisdom. For one thing, the culture in which I grew up, and my training and conditioning as a communicator of the faith, never took that perspective into account. For the most part, many of the sermons I preached were commendably traditional in content and style, suited to the experiences and tastes of middle-class congregations. To be sure, I recognized there were more angular testimonies to the truth, laced with images and language quite alien to the ways of comfortable, well-dressed suburban worshipers, but reference to them were likely to be offensive and would probably be misunderstood. Besides, I kept hearing, as most ministers hear, that during the week people have plenty of exposure to the darker sides of the human venture, and, come Sunday, they are entitled to discourses that ring the changes on inspiration and ennoblement. Much of this time I conformed to such expectations, mindful, above all, that I had been called to be the conveyer of good news, of a Word that sees beyond the misery and tragedy of the times to a triumph of the Spirit.

But now, when I recall services of worship I conducted in the earlier years of my ministry, when I shuffle through files of old sermons (a dispiriting experience at best), I have an odd sense of spiritual irrelevancy. What I read sounds so appropriately upbeat, so terribly elevating, so properly moral, so thoroughly antiseptic. It sounds like an ecclesiastical version of *The Sound of Music,* that tuneful and frightfully wholesome paean to uprightness. (I recall the member of the congregation who considered it as a corollary to the New Testament and who was put out with me because of my refusal to recommend that "Climb Every Mountain" be added to our choir's repertory.)

Services of worship were meticulously ordered, especially those of the Lord's Supper. I can still see deacons tramping down the aisle in lockstep precision. I can see my associate and me carefully synchronizing our movements about the table and deaconesses laying out the elements, measuring with a ruler to a half inch the distance between the plates of bread and the chalice! And there was the deacon who objected to the minister breaking a loaf instead of lifting the tray of tiny cubes of Wonder Bread—thereby avoiding the unsightliness, he said, of crumbs on the chancel carpet!

More seriously, what went on was, I am afraid, a protective covering against harsh realities festering beneath our well-groomed exteriors. Were we contriving to conceal our hurts from one another? Was I helping to erect a barrier against a suspected menace? We knew of the angry but muted muttering in the dark pockets of our society, but, it was hoped upbeat spiritual chatter could hold it at bay. Now and then I would speak a prophetic word, but somehow it didn't quite come off in authentic prophetic style.

Søren Kierkegaard once related an instance of this.

> In the magnificent cathedral, the elect favorite of the fashionable world appears before an elect company and preaches with emotion upon the text he himself elected: "God hath elected the base things of the world, and the things that are despised"—and nobody laughs![2]

What we keep forgetting is how clearly the Bible in its exposures of the truth is tipped toward what is foolish and weak, what is lowly and despised. How odd it is that the dark underside of human experience is often where we have our clearest understanding of grace!

If my experience is anything to go by, that certainly has been true for me. I testify to the mysterious working of grace at the center of my own struggling up out of the darkness toward the light of self-ownership and of becoming a more authentic person. As Dag Hammarskjöld said once, it's the "night side" of one's being forced into the light by the pressure of grace. Here on the evening slant to my days, I understand much more about their "night side" and about the tragic dimension to all our lives. For the most part, however, our Western culture refuses to take such a dimension very seriously. It may be grudgingly acknowledged that a tragic element shows up now and then. If it does, we assume that (1) it can be satisfactorily handled by the insights and disciplines of depth psychology and treated therapeutically; or (2) it can be attacked by human ingenuity and skills in engineering and, if not eradicated, at least drastically reduced; or (3) in stoical Puritan style, it is simply to be endured, life is to be faced with raw courage in the face of a hostile universe.

All this has a certain validity about it and cannot be cavalierly dismissed, but it is strangely unsatisfying for those who take seriously biblical faith, which insists that there is a fundamental, bone-deep flaw in us. As Graham Greene said once, we are implicated in some terrible, aboriginal calamity. "For I do not do the good I want, but the evil I do not want is what I do. Now if I do what I do not want, it is no longer I that do it, but sin which dwells within me [Romans 7:19,20]." Call it "original sin" or anything you like. All I know is that it is an elemental ingredient in my makeup as a human being!

Eugene O'Neill's play *Long Day's Journey Into Night* is

an exploration of the "night side" of the author and his family. It is evidence of the fact that often the most sensitive and effective communicators of the truth are those who take the risk of revealing with unflinching honesty the circumstances that shaped their existence and their outlook on the human scene. The play was in his blood for years. It haunted him, he said, and he had to write it. It is about the O'Neills when Eugene was a young man, at a time of crisis in their tormented life as a family. It is about people living in the most intimate of circumstances but who, despite an innate compassion they feel for one another, cannot speak of it or show it.

The play reacquaints us with the full dimensions of our humanity. Compassionately, tenderly, lovingly, O'Neill probes the darkness in the lives of four tragically unhappy people, and from what he finds he draws his conclusions about the human venture: that it is a trap, a blind alley, a mindless mystery, a seascape shrouded in fog, treacherous and deceiving—a long day's journey into night. It's view is about as far as you can get from the New Testament!

What is a responsible reaction of a person of Christian faith to a work that is poles apart from Christianity's buoyant, hopeful affirmations? One thing is to admit that in such a play we have placed before us, skillfully, with all the power of a great artist, the raw material to which the good news of the love of God is always addressed. It is done far more eloquently and realistically than many a minister's pedestrian homiletical efforts. We are reminded that it is in the depths of our being that God is to be found, or, more accurately, that it is in experiences of degradation and desperation that God is most likely to find us, to speak to us, to heal us. *Long Day's Journey Into Night* can scarcely be called a "Christian" play. Nonetheless, it depicts the human situation in such a way that the gospel can win a readier hearing. (Perhaps we shouldn't expect more than that of any sermon!)

But even in O'Neill, in spite of his long-range conclusions, there are intimations of light beyond the darkness, clearing skies beyond the fog, that somewhere out past our groping for meaning, there is a place to catch hold. There is more than a hint of it in his dedication of the play to his wife, Carlotta.

> For Carlotta, on our twelfth wedding anniversary: Dearest: I give you the original script of the play of old sorrow written in tears and in blood. A sadly inappropriate gift, it would seem, for a day celebrating happiness. But you will understand. I mean it as a tribute to your love and tenderness which gave me the faith in love that enabled me to face my dead at last and write this play—write it with deep pity and understanding and forgiveness for all the four haunted Tyrones. These twelve years, Beloved One, have been a journey into light—into love. Gene[3]

That isn't the gospel, but it's a piece of it, and perhaps that's all we can ask at times! It's a step at least toward the faith we profess, that by the grace of God, life is steadily becoming what the New Testament insists it can be for each of us, and what it sings about all the way through—a long night's journey into day!

Secular Variations on Sacred Themes

"When grace doesn't come from the center, it comes from the circumference."

Call her Judy. She attended Sunday morning worship occasionally, but I didn't really get to know her until she joined a play-reading group the church had organized. One evening we were working on Arthur Miller's *Death of a Salesman*. She was reading Linda Loman's lines. I sensed a growing undercurrent of emotion. We got to Linda's heartbreaking speech in defense of Willy. "He's not the finest character that ever lived. But he's a human being, and a terrible thing is happening to him. So attention must be paid. . . . Attention, attention must be finally paid to such a person." Judy began to cry softly, excused herself, and left the room.

She came to see me the next day to apologize, as she felt she should, and to explain. The trouble, she said, was that her father was a carbon copy of Willy Loman—a man "with the wrong dreams—all, all wrong." Like Willy, he never knew who he was. He exploited his wife and his children, kept them at such a distance that any show of genuine affection was impossible. And he took his own life. There was little for me to do but to listen while the dam broke. One thing came of it: Like Eugene O'Neill, Judy was better able to face her dead, which also for some of us may be a piece of unfinished business.

Carl was another member of the congregation. I had a telephone call from him late one night. He was in his hotel room in New York. He had just come in from a performance of *J.B.*, Archibald MacLeish's play based on the story of Job, and he said he wanted to talk to me. Here, too, plugged up feelings were let loose. It wasn't, as in Judy's case, an emotional crisis but rather a sense of release, a realization that there were depths to his being he had never tried to plumb. There was territory he now needed to explore—questions about evil and suffering, spiritual barrenness, the loneliness of not being listened to or taken seriously.

Again, the "Beyond in our midst," the mystery pressing close, an opening for grace through an unsuspected medium, quite outside certified locales or channels: hymns, prayers, sermons, anthems, hushed silence, candles, and stained glass. "When grace doesn't come from the center, it comes from the circumference."

The most eloquent and determining movement of grace into my life came, precisely, from the circumference, from a pattern of experience outside the "normal" configurations of human relationships. Talk about surprises!

It came about when our daughter owned to herself, and then to us, the truth about her sexual orientation—that she was a lesbian, that all her relationships from there on out would be built around that basic, undeniable fact. Needless to say, we, her parents, were surprised, suddenly faced with an aspect of human behavior about which we knew practically nothing. Nonetheless, in our limbolike state, with a number of things to be sorted out, Eleonore and I quickly took care of two responses. The first, and the most important, was to make clear to Loey that whatever was implied in her disclosure, there was no way in which it could possibly affect our relationship to her as her parents. "Love is not love which alters when it alteration finds" (Shakespeare, Sonnet CXVI). We made it clear that she was the same lively, lovable young woman of poise and integrity five minutes after her disclosure that she had been five minutes before it. Our second resolution was to find out all we could about homosexuality, and we recognized that there was much to learn.

Along with reading and discussions, our most valuable learnings have come through our firsthand association with Loey's friends, members of "support groups" that have seen her through dark times. Our relationships with them have stretched our minds, widened our affections, and hastened our maturity. We now know, if we know anything, that homosexuality is not a medical or psychological disorder; that homosexuals are not, ipso facto, promiscuous perverts or child molestors; that they are not sinners before God needing only to repent of their wickedness. While a lot remains to be discovered about homosexuality and its root causes, we do accept the widely held belief that it is not a way of life that is chosen by an individual but is something to be acknowledged as a given fact in that person's makeup. While it is true that in the Bible there are several strong injunctions against homosexual behavior, they have to do with the difficult task of preserving the purity of both Old Testament and New Testament religion against the seductive encroachments of paganism. The Bible reveals nothing of the modern psychological understanding of homosexuality as one expression of human sexuality in general.

Most significantly, we are convinced that homophobia (the fear, even terror, of homosexuality) is the major stumbling block in the way of a loving, open acceptance of lesbians and gay men into the normal give-and-take of relationships in human society.

Our lives have been enriched by two special marks of grace in our experience of being parents of a homosexual. One is simply being moved by the raw courage it takes publicly to identify oneself as such in a society where hostility or ignorance, or both, are the commonplace reactions. Our daughter has known unspeakable pain in experiences of rejection in the course of fulfilling her vocation, regrettable and ironic since she is an ordained minister in a faith that is constantly reminding the world that "all are one in Christ." Still in a pioneer period, she carries on with what Roger Hazelton properly calls "graceful courage." One day, precisely because of God's grace flowing through her and many others, the place of homosexual men and women in our society and in our churches will be secure and honored.

A second evidence of grace marking our experience is how obviously our lives have been enriched through the friendships we have made in the homosexual communities we have been privileged to know. While lesbians and gay men are subject to the same vagaries, lapses in judgment, and foolishness the rest of us have to put up with, there is, nonetheless, a kind of purity and intensity of commitment about them—the mark of all those in our society who are forever having to fight their way upstream in order to claim their right to be who they are against adverse currents of ignorance, bigotry, and fear.

I confess to a strange but creative tension building up in me in these evening years. On the one hand, the older I grow, the more fully I understand the orthodox affirmations of New Testament faith, Pauline theology, pure and simple: the gift of new life in the middle of old; unmerited, unearned grace flooding dry, barren spaces; the experience of being "saved," if you will. In one sense, speaking theologically, I have become more conservative. On the other hand, I become more and more appreciative of and grateful for the insights of a purely secular reading of life. I have been strengthened and enriched by affirmations of the truth made by artists who have no affiliation whatever with the church or any formal ordering of religion. Grace from the circumference! Consequently, as a discipline in discerning and voicing the truth, I try to keep eyes and ears open to all kinds of secular variations on sacred themes.

The soundest authority I have found for it is the Bible itself. For one thing, it never assumes or talks about *two* worlds—a purified, rarefied "sacred" world, peopled by saints and other "spiritual" types, on the one hand, and on the other, a "secular" order of being where a questionable mode of creation is played out. The Bible takes a strictly holistic stance. In the story of creation, for example, it tells how God painstakingly shaped the world, stood back, looked it over, and pronounced the whole thing good— roses and ragweed, zephyrs and tornadoes, lush jungles and barren deserts.

Moreover, as far as the human scene is concerned, God wasn't nearly as fussy as we are about the people chosen to guarantee a royal line of succession. Take Jacob, for example, there in the Book of Genesis, as wily a con man as you will find, scarcely a model in morality for children and youth. Why blessing was bestowed on a liar and a cheat is God's private business, not ours. Or there's David, the most popular, best-loved king Israel ever had, one eye on the covenant, the other on the lovely Bathsheba. Then there are the prophets with their head-on defiance of the sanctified practices of established religion and their outrageous proposition that to punish the faithlessness of the nation, God was using godless, pagan nations such as the Babylonians and the Assyrians!

There is Isaiah's record of God's plaintive appeal: "I was ready to be sought by those who did not ask for me; I was ready to be found by those who did not seek me. I said,

'Here am I, here am I,' to a nation that did not call on my name [Isaiah 65:1]." Or remember Jesus' words: "And I have other sheep that are not of this fold [John 10:16]."

Nothing is "secular" to God, said William Temple once. If this is so, to "do" theology—that is, not simply talk about it in sermons and seminars—we Christians shall have to become very familiar with the "secular" scene, the world outside our altars and prayer books. It means taking it seriously, probing it, dealing with it in such a way that what is spiritually implicit in it becomes explicit. It means exploring it with respect and reverence in order that its holiness may be recognized, often in startling, provocative ways. More and more these days we must learn to look for transcendence in and through the secular, finding the marks of grace, however crooked and perverse they may appear, and not just in a spiritual process authenticated by the church or tradition.

Monica Furlong has strong language on the subject, for example, of Christians being at home in the contemporary arts. She observes how many church people there are who walk through the pastures of modern writing, missing the honesty and the courage of its humanism and complaining that God is not obviously praised. She believes that by such standards a poor novel, simply because it is written by a Christian, is better than some pagan celebration of life, or a TV program that is a bland interpretation of Christian faith is considered better than one where people express the inhibitions that hold them back from God.

A lively dialogue between faith and the arts is one of the necessary ingredients in the development of a sturdy "life in the Spirit." The necessity, or the propriety, of such a dialogue has been debated for centuries. Tertullian, an early church Father, asked a critical question: "What has Athens to do with Jerusalem?" Until fairly recently, on the American scene, the answer has largely been, "Not much." There are reasons for this, of course. One has been a general suspicion of artists. They are often thought of as ethereal, fragile creatures, cloistered and cushioned in some precious world of their own, while the rest of us slug things out against the hard-nosed realities of a competitive society. For many Americans, art is largely a luxury to be enjoyed in leisure time, after the bills have been paid. It is not in the mainstream of muscular, extrovert America, shaped by a husky, "frontier" model and not by an effete cultural tradition imported from Europe.

For another thing, we have to keep in mind how strongly our Puritan ancestry has conditioned us. I realize now how strongly it conditioned me. The cultural climate of our home when I was growing up was definitely on the arid side. It was like living below the eastern face of a North American mountain range, like the Rockies or the Cascades. By the time the prevailing winds of the arts—music, literature, painting—reached us, they had dropped most of their cultural moisture on the western slopes, with only an occasional shower left for our stark, desertlike terrain. The music we cranked out on our ancient Columbia Graphaphone was limited to Sousa marches, sentimental ballads, or Kettelby's romantic imagery of a Persian market or a monastery garden. Books recommended for Sunday afternoon reading, an integral part of our Sabbath observance, were signed out from the Sunday school library. Most of them, in dreary, mustard-color jackets, were tales of boys and girls who, because of exemplary moral conduct, persevered through many misfortunes and won their parents' approbation with sickening regularity. Their literary style was a mix of the adventures of the Bobbsey twins and the *Encyclopedia Britannica*. In the graphic arts, we got no further than the colored lithographs of Sunday school leaflets.

Our Puritan fathers and mothers were never quite as dour and unworldly as often depicted. Nonetheless, their stance toward society and culture still has to be reckoned with. Essentially, it was unremitting contention—faith against "the world," spirit against the flesh. In addition, a deadly serious work ethic left little time or room for the kind of sitting loose, even abandon, which is necessary for a real appreciation and enjoyment of the work of artists.

Again, many Americans have given more attention to the rational, "head" side of us than to the "heart." On encountering a piece of work by an artist—a painting, let's say, or a poem—our tendency, straight off, is to try to think our way into its meaning rather than allowing it to say something to our emotions, which, after all are what a poem addresses.

Two further observations. When art is introduced into an enterprise, it is thought of primarily, by many Americans, of having a utilitarian function. Art can be *useful*, we believe, in illustrating moral and spiritual concepts. If artists are to be taken seriously, put them to work! God forgive me the times I have done just that, foraged for a good poem to bolster my argument, drafted Shakespeare or Emily Dickinson to shore up a badly sagging section of a sermon. Or we limit our choice of art to traditional subject matter, to themes and situations that are readily recognizable as "religious." It's that way in the entertainment world. At the drop of the parson's hat, people will flock in droves to a "beard and bathrobe" epic, having been assured that they are in for a towering spiritual experience.

Happily, in recent years Americans have been returning to an earlier alliance. Art and artists are being taken more seriously, thanks, in part, to the communications media. Works of art, classical and contemporary, are available to the majority of Americans, not just to those who can afford forty or fifty dollars for a seat to a play or an opera. A new, brisk dialogue is going on between "secular" artists and church folk. The longer they talk, the plainer it becomes that if the gospel is to have a hearing, it must have a worldly authenticity about it. It must be in touch with people where and as they are, many of whom haven't the slightest familiarity with the church and the Christian tradition. It also means knowing that, like us, they wrestle with the same elemental questions about human existence: meaning, purpose, pain, suffering, death, and redemption. There are many eloquent, passionate explorations of these themes out on the other side of the stained glass, and we had best be familiar with them. We may not agree with everything we hear, no more than we do with what many fellow-Christians have to say. It may even be that some of the conversations we have will turn out to be more fruitful than a lot of the in-house debates on matters of no great consequence that we find time for.

Persuaded of this, it became my practice to preach a summertime series of sermons, theological commentaries on novels and plays that I had discovered were mines of spiritual insights well worth the digging.

In singling out the following writers, I make no claims about their place in literary history. Nor do I imply that their work is immortal. What I submit is a sampler, novels, plays, poetry that I have found to be searching explorations of essentially spiritual or "sacred" themes. Obviously, the selection reflects my own temperament and tastes, my own dilemmas and delights. It may, however, prompt others to be on the watch for revelations of the Spirit in their own reading.

In fiction, there is Graham Greene with, as he put it, his obsession with the workings of God's grace in a world tainted through and through with evil. He dramatizes the familiar "hound of heaven" theme, the grace of God pursuing people straight up to the gates of hell. There is *The Power and the Glory, The Heart of the Matter, The Human Factor*, and in a somewhat different vein, *Monsignor Quixote*, a delightful retelling of Cervantes's classical tale in the adventures and growing bond of friendship and love between a priest who has begun to have serious doubts about his faith, and a Communist politician.

There is Alan Paton creating on the tortured terrain of his native South Africa such compassionate and tender portrayals of the human spirit as we find in *Ah, But Your Land Is Beautiful* and his earlier *Cry, the Beloved County*. There are

Saul Bellow's *Herzog* and *Mr. Sammler's Planet*. John Cheever's *Collected Stories* are indelible etchings of Americans trying to cope with the comforts, the respectability, the emptiness, and the moral temptations of suburbia, which was the locale of a sizable portion of my ministry. In a radical shift of scene, his novel *Falconer* is a parable of the search for redemption in the setting of a prison.

There is John Updike with his series of *Rabbit* novels and Flannery O'Connor with her implacable and passionately held belief that what is wrong with contemporary society, purely and simply, is that it has turned its back on its spiritual foundations, which, for her, are summed up in the basic tenets of Roman Catholic theology. As a result, she insists, the world has become a grotesque, demon-ridden place, and its salvation lies in a radical dependence on the grace of God. Her thesis is powerfully played out in *Everything That Rises Must Converge* and *The Violent Bear It Away*. In Peter DeVries's novels we have laughter turned into a secular sacrament, but in the one interruption in a cascade of hilarity, we have his heartbreaking novel *The Blood of the Lamb*. It is a touching and revealing exposé of a father's heart engulfed by the death of his twelve-year-old daughter, and we shall examine it later in more detail.

In drama, there are Edward Albee's *A Delicate Balance*, MacLeish's *J.B.*, Miller's *Death of a Salesman*, and Tennessee Williams's *Night of the Iguana*. *A Man for All Seasons*, Robert Bolt's play about Sir Thomas More; *Rosencrantz and Guildenstern Are Dead*, in which Tom Stoppard stands Shakespeare's *Hamlet* on its head with fascinating results; *Our Town* by Thornton Wilder; *Rhinoceros* by Eugene Ionesco; and *Equus* by Peter Shaffer are other spiritually revealing plays.

There are poems in which singular insights into the life of the Spirit may lie undetected until a second or third reading flushes them to the surface: "Churchgoing," by Philip Larkin; Sylvia Plath's "Black Rook in Rainy Weather;" Richard Wilbur's "Love Calls Us to the Things of This

World;" Dylan Thomas's "Do Not Go Gentle Into That Good Night;" W.H. Auden's "For the Time Being." There are Robert Frost's sombre ponderings on the dark side of the human venture: "Acquainted with the Night" "Desert Places," "Tree at My Window," "An Old Man's Winter Night," or, in another mood, one of his greatest poems, "Directive."

There is Robinson Jeffers's "The World's Wonders" and Edwin Arlington Robinson's "The Prodigal Son," a revealing commentary on Jesus' parable. Howard Nemerov offers biting satire in "Boom!," a spoof of the annual "Miss America" circus in Atlantic City. William Carlos Williams's "Tract" will likely lead to some sobering thoughts on "the American way of death." And for satire etched in pure acid, Dorothy Parker has no equal: "Bohemia," "Inventory." In a gentler mood, there is Phyllis McGinley, for example, "A Gallery of Elders," and Gwendolyn Brooks, whose "Lovers of the Poor" should be read carefully by church women's societies and other organizations committed to bestowing largess on the poor, "the very, very worthy poor." For social commentary couched in laughter, there is nothing quite like Ogden Nash's "The Seven Spiritual Stages of Mrs. Marmaduke Moore."

To be specific, consider a couple of poems in detail.

For the first, go back to the nineteenth century. Gerard Manley Hopkins has a timeless quality about him, and like Emily Dickinson, he broke traditional molds and helped pave the way for a lot of present-day verse. His poems are not always the easiest to read, but true art requires an investment on our part, some digging before it yields its treasure. "God's Grandeur," except for some curious word twisting here and there, is plain enough, once we grant poets their freedom to play with words, as a painter plays with color. Without that freedom, they may just as well settle for no-nonsense, everyday prose. Read the poem slowly, out loud, allowing its images to flicker across the screen of your mind. Let the power inherent in its special use of words have its way with you.

> The world is charged with the grandeur of God.
> It will flame out, like shining from shook foil;
> It gathers to a greatness, like the ooze of oil
> Crushed. Why do men then not reck his rod?
> Generations have trod, have trod, have trod;
> All is seared with trade; bleared, smeared with toil;
> And wears man's smudge and shares man's smell:
>   the soil
> Is bare now, nor can foot feel, being shod.
> And for all this, nature is never spent;
> There lives the dearest freshness deep down things;
> And though the last lights off the black West went
> Oh, morning, at the brown brink eastward, springs—
> Because the Holy Ghost over the bent
> World broods with warm breast and with ah!
>   bright wings.[4]

There is Anne Sexton's book of poems the *Awful Rowing Toward God*. It is a prime example of a "secular variation on a sacred theme." Sexton lived most of her life in suburban Boston. At one time, she taught English literature. She was married, had two children, was divorced. Never part of the life of a church, like Graham Greene she was, nonetheless, haunted by the major themes of the Christian faith. She did her writing in its back yard, so to speak. A text for her life might well be the cry of a distraught man to Jesus, "Lord, I believe; help my unbelief!" She said once, "There is a hard-core part of me that believes, and there's this little critic in me that believes nothing."

There is more to be gained in listening to those whose faith journey has been tortured than we suspect. We may be uncomfortable in their presence. Their suffering may embarrass us, their honesty disturb us, their language, at times, shock us. We may not accept all their conclusions about meaning or faith, but out of identifying ourselves as closely as we can with their experience and pain may come a tighter hold on our own lives and a curious kind of joy. Sexton has been called a "confessional poet." That is to say, the raw stuff of her inner life became the chief ingredient of her verse. But for all the rawness, several factors make it considerably more than wallowing in ugliness or slumming down the back alleys of an unhappy life. For one thing, we are aware of a constant, relentless groping toward the light, a stubborn refusal simply to surrender to the powers of darkness. Sexton had more than one occasion to do so, being subject to spells of depression and despair. For another, her writing serves as a catharsis: turning wounds into words. Or again, we recognize that Sexton is talking about a universal pain—yours and mine, perhaps. So we are led to say, "If Anne Sexton can hope, perhaps *we* can hope!"

But the most important thing to keep in mind about Sexton's poetry is its constant drift toward transcendence, which, in its way, is more important than whether she ever found fully what she searched for so stubbornly and poignantly. *The Awful Rowing Toward God* is about just that. She uses the metaphor of rowing a small boat, tying together the first and last poems in the book. The first, simply called "Rowing," states the situation. "I am still rowing," she tells us, after describing her struggling efforts. There follows a series of poems reflecting, among other things, on her bouts with depression and loneliness. In the final poem, "The Rowing Endeth," following a treacherous passage across open water against head winds and adverse current, she makes a safe landing and there experiences the surprise of her life!

> I'm mooring my rowboat
> at the dock of the island called God.
> This dock is made in the shape of a fish
> and there are many boats moored
> at many different docks.
> "It's okay," I say to myself,
> with blisters that broke and healed
> and broke and healed—
> saving themselves over and over.
> And salt sticking to my face and arms like

> a glue-skin pocked with grains of tapioca.
> I empty myself from my wooden boat
> And onto the flesh of the Island.
>
> "On with it!" He says and thus
> we squat on the rocks by the sea
> and play—can it be true—
> a game of poker.
> He calls me.
> I win because I hold a royal straight flush.
> He wins because He holds five aces.
> A wild card had been announced
> but I had not heard it
> being in such a state of awe
> when He took out the cards and dealt.
> As He plunks down His five aces
> and I sit grinning at my royal flush,
> He starts to laugh,
> the laughter rolling like a hoop out of His mouth
> and into mine,
> and such laughter that He doubles right over me
> laughing a Rejoice-Chorus at our two triumphs.
> Then I laugh, the fishy dock laughs.
> The Absurd laughs.
> Dearest dealer,
> I with my royal straight flush,
> love you so for your wild card,
> that untamable, eternal, gut-driven *ha-ha*
> and lucky love.[5]

Clearly, all of this, more than once, has been about me. I have felt quite at home in an odd-ball poker game like that one there on the dock—that owning of "two triumphs." First, there was my own sense of winning. Looking back over the years of ministry, I see there were times when I could affirm my own royal flush and what I was able to do with it—heal hurts, ease pain, help troubled people sort out a tangled skein and pick up their work again, speak a clear word in a time of confusion, strike fire in the cold. But I was aware, as well, of another Presence, and I was grateful beyond measure for that element of mystery that now and then stood whatever I had achieved on its head. I have felt affirmed but also humbled by a wisdom so vastly wiser than my own—that unbelievable, unexpected, undeserved "wild card"—God's fifth ace!

Greene, Cheever, O'Connor, Auden, Frost, Sexton, and all the others—these are voices blowing in the wind of our time. If we care about maintaining a lively dialogue between them and biblical faith—and there really is no other sensible choice—they deserve a respectful hearing. Church folk spend far too much time talking only to one another. We need the discipline of dialogue, especially with those who will not accept facile answers to the brutal questions that are asked at the brink of meaninglessness. We can be enormously enriched by keeping in close touch with those who have left insulated spiritual cloisters and standing with them in the cross fire of contemporary life and culture, however bewildered we may be at first by what we hear and see. We shall learn something of the anguish of the disinherited and the despairing, to weep when they weep, to cry out at times with their torturing doubts, without feeling a necessity to furnish them with advice or a package of answers for their questions.

In his essay "The Gospel as Tragedy," Frederick Beuchner speaks eloquently of the link between tragedy and the good news of the love of God in Jesus Christ. He remembers King Lear out in the storm on the heath, tearing off his clothes as if, in the recognition of his madness, he knows that if there is ever to be healing and a true sheltering for any of us, it is with our nakedness and helplessness that it has to start. And says he,

> that is where anyone who preaches the Gospel has to start, too. After the silence that is truth comes the news that is bad before it is good, the word that is tragedy before it is comedy because it strips us bare in order ultimately to

clothe us. . . . The sheltering word can be spoken only after the word that leaves us without a roof over our heads, the answering word only after the word it answers.[6]

I think back, uneasily, to the times, either in preaching or pastoral counseling, when I offered an answering word before the word it was supposed to answer had been spoken, before an awkward, unavoidable question with all its unsettling implications had been asked. Like the times I have exploited poetry, without taking into account the anguish that the poet must honestly have tried to face, without a few stark sentences spoken to precipitate the tears before a healing hand can be felt. Or I think of the sermons I preached that reached a climax in a reference to the cross of Christ without any intimation of the horror and degradation of death by crucifixion. The answer before the question!

So my journey has advanced—circumscribed by mystery, startled by surprise, set off balance at times by absurdity: the grace of God showing up in the least likely, most unsuspected places. I've not always properly appreciated such strange invasions, but the more often I experience them, the more aware I become that I am never far from a caring and a love that is unconditional. "Amazing grace": It is the only adequate metaphor for understanding my homecomings!

CHAPTER 4

Wonders of the Journey

> Wonder is a word to wonder about. It contains a mixture of messages: something marvelous and miraculous, surprising, raising unanswerable questions about itself.
>
> —Lewis Thomas

Every civilization and culture celebrates its own special wonders. There were, for instance, the Seven Wonders of the Ancient World: The pyramids of Egypt, the hanging gardens of Babylon, the statue of Zeus at Olympia, and the rest.

The eminent pathologist Lewis Thomas, in his book *Late Night Thoughts on Listening to Mahler's Ninth Symphony*, was asked to join several others to name the seven wonders of the modern world. Along with several "miraculous" phenomena of biology and physiology, he came up with these: termites, a human child, and the planet earth itself.

I tried my hand at a list of my own: the snow peaks of the high Himalayas, the Amazon River, Shakespeare's sonnets, Verdi's *Falstaff,* Wagner's *Die Meistersinger,* Bach's *The Passion According to St. Matthew,* the fifteenth chapter of the Gospel of Mark, and Dylan Thomas's *A Child's Christmas in Wales*. Also a Bengal tiger, the thunder of surf on an outer beach, the people who stubbornly have gone on loving me whether I deserved it or not, and the gaunt, high courage of men and women whose lives bear testimony to the claims of another world beyond this one. That's more than seven, I know, but that's the nature of wonder; it's always spilling over our careful calculations!

Whatever gets on the list, wonder itself is the key to the selections. Thomas says, "Wonder is a word to wonder about. It contains a mixture of messages: something marvelous and miraculous, surprising, raising unanswerable questions about itself." Years ago, Thoreau wrote in the same vein.

> In wildness is the preservation of the world.... We need the tonic of wildness.... At the same time that we are earnest to explore and learn all things, we require that all things be mysterious and unexplorable, that land and sea be infinitely wild, unsurveyed and unfathomed by us because unfathomable.... We need to witness our own limits transgressed, and some life pasturing freely where we never wander.[1]

I keep asking myself the question: What and where are the places, the situations, the experiences that give me scalp-tingling delight and that have intimations of meaning beyond what the poet Richard Wilbur calls "the punctual rape of every blessed day"? Where are the pastures in which I have never wandered? Are there sounds I have heard that echo with the music of distant singing, that pierce the thick casing of daily obligations and rituals, that tempt me to unbolt a door I've not dared to open?

Lately, I have been taking a sightseeing tour across my own inner terrain, with a number of side trips into unexplored territory. I recognize, of course, that in a practical, hard-nosed kind of way, like most people, I can get by without any "tonic of wildness." I can settle for an honorable, perfectly respectable life, crammed with doing my duty and good works, earning, perhaps, a B for carrying through on what is expected of me. The trouble is that now and then, in off moments, in the dark of a sleepless hour, perhaps, it occurs to me that my days are becoming plodding and pedestrian, without lilt or fire or any dancing of the Spirit, and that I have become so hemmed in by the relentless regularity of chores and appointments that there can be no expectation of hearing voices or having to stop to investigate a bush flaming at the roadside.

Rainer Maria Rilke's startling poem "Archaic Torso of Apollo" keeps haunting me. Moved by his metaphor, I find myself sauntering through the sculpture gallery of an art museum and suddenly coming upon a treasure from the ancient world.

> We did not know his legendary head,
> in which the eyeballs ripened. But
> his torso still glows like a candelabrum
> in which his gaze, only turned low,
>
> holds and gleams. Else could not the curve
> of the breast blind you, nor in the slight turn
> of the loins could a smile be running
> to that middle, which carried procreation.
>
> Else would this stone be standing maimed and short
> below the shoulders' translucent plunge
> nor glimmering like the fell of beasts of prey
>
> nor breaking out of all its contours
> like a star: for there is no place
> that does not see you. You must change your life.[2]

There is an urgency about it: to stay alive, fully human, we must "witness our own limits transgressed," to be in the presence of things "infinitely wild, unsurveyed and unfathomed by us, because unfathomable." There is a particular poignancy about it for me, here in the later days of my years. It is all the more important for me to be pulled up short and to be required to contemplate the shape, the direction, the rhythms of the time I have left. Herewith, then, a brief rundown of the wonders that have given a special luster to my journey.

The Poetic Stance

Poetry is the best enabler I know for getting at and telling the truth. After fifty years of sermons, preaching them from the pulpit and now listening to them in the pew, after all the speeches I've heard, the books and articles I've read, I am totally convinced that nothing is ever effectively communicated unless preachers, speakers, and writers have learned to rely on poetry. Let me make clear what I mean by poetry. I do not mean a lot of fancy, purplish language. I do not necessarily mean verse, rhymed or unrhymed. What I do mean is a poetic stance, recognizing the unique quality and function of the poetic as a mode of language rather than a particular literary form. I mean that to communicate something in fullness and depth, the precious qualities of poetry are required—metaphor, rhythm, the selection of one set of words over against another, and their arrangement.

But what is *poetry*? Although that is largely an unanswerable, "unfathomable" question, we must make a stab at it. Certainly, any attempt at an answer has to begin by simply taking for granted the awesome power of words. For all the sophistication of the electronic media, awesome in itself, words are still our basic coinage for communication. I am forever being dismayed by how cavalierly so many people mishandle and abuse them. They operate on the blasphemous principle that one word will serve as well as another. But, said Frederick Buechner once, to name a thing—and that is what we do when we preach, speak or write—is to know it in a new and powerful way. So, he said, let those who "name things" beware because in so doing they are wielding a great power that can be a matter of life and death. What he means is that speaking and writing is not simply an exercise in word usage; it is a kind of priestly craft that involves a special discipline.

There is a danger in all of this, namely, semantic inflation—putting too much stock in the words themselves. I am guilty of it at times, having "a thing," as I do, about words, and certain people whose opinions I respect do not hesitate to call me on it. It is the temptation to exploit words as playthings instead of putting them to work, to substitute simply a clever arrangement of them for substance. It is a fairly common occupational hazard for preachers. We'll do well to keep in mind Thomas Carlyle's devastating comment about a celebrated London preacher of his time. If one day, said Carlyle, he were to find something to say, he certainly would know how to say it!

For all of that, I come down hard on this privilege granted us, to use the English language, and when I do, to remember that I wield awesome power. I am mindful of the holy, symbolic quality of words, their capacity to bless, to burn, to terrify, to throw open doors onto the truth, and I know how dependent I am upon them to speak of unspeakable things. It is the difference between a technician and a creative craftsperson, the difference, let's say, between a photographer who snaps likenesses for passports and a portrait painter. I fear that too many of the sermons I have listened to—and preached—are of the "passport" variety.

There is an elementary lesson in the use of language, saying something about simplicity and conciseness, in the correspondence between a certain New England plumber and one of the research bureaus in Washington. Working on a job, this plumber was having a lot of trouble with clogged pipes, and he wrote to ask whether he should use sulfuric acid to clear out the system. He received a lengthy, convoluted reply, larded with technical jargon. Unable to make sense of it, he wrote again, with the same results. With the admirable persistence of the widow in the New Testament, he wrote a third letter. This time his inquiry reached the hands of a discerning staff member who promptly shot back a terse note: "Don't use sulfuric acid; it eats the hell out of the pipes!"

"I preach coarsely: that giveth content to all," said Martin Luther once. "Hebrew and Latin I spare until we learned ones come together, and then we make it so curled and finical that even God wondereth at us." To speak, to preach, to write coarsely, that is to say simply, plainly, cleanly, is to be taken for granted. But it is only the beginning, for prose has lamentable limitations. It can say just so much but no more. Hence, the "poetic stance." So, back to the question: What is poetry?

In a way, it *is* an unanswerable question. Try to define poetry in prose, and you end up with language that is its antithesis. After several frustrating attempts at definition, one poet gave up and simply said, "Poetry is the stuff that poets write." To understand what it is, you have to use poetry's own unique devices: random observations, flashes of insight, bits and pieces, and, above all, metaphor, which my unabridged Webster says is "a figure of speech in which one thing is likened to another, different thing by being spoken of as if it were that other."

Emily Dickinson said once that when she had finished reading a real poem, she had the feeling that the top of her head had been blown off. William Butler Yeats said that poetry is "blood, imagination, and intellect running together." Robert Frost called it "a performance in words," and on another occasion, "something that begins in delight and ends in wisdom." For A.E. Housman, it was "a shiver down the spine, a contraction of the throat, a precipitation of water to the eyes, a sensation in the pit of the stomach."

When Marianne Moore talked about poetry she did it, consistently, in a poem. Whatever else poetry is, she said, it is the place for the "genuine."

> Hands that can grasp, eyes
> that can dilate, hair that can rise
> if it must, those things are important not because a
> high-sounding interpretation can be put upon them but
> because they are useful. . . .
> (Not) till the poets among us can be
> literalists of the imagination . . .

and can present
for inspection imaginary gardens with real toads in
in them shall we have it.[3]

However you say it, poetry is heightened, multidimensional language that encompasses imagination and reality in the same breath and immediately engages a person's heart and feelings. By its unique, even outrageous, combination of words, it shamelessly manipulates our imagination so that we find ourselves participating in ideas and situations we may never have dealt with before. This is contrary to an inherited and wrong-headed bias about poetry, that it is an airy escape from reality, an ethereal contemplation of beauty over the clink of teacups, far removed from the rowdy realities of every day. Actually, poetry is one of the toughest means of communication there is. It calls the shots. It dredges the ugly bottom of human experience. It stands sometimes at the outer limits of experience and can scare the hell out of us! It comes into being at the intersection of our lives where imagination stumbles upon reality, or vice versa, and exposes and illuminates reality in such a way that we are never quite the same again.

What I am testifying to is how often for me, poetry has been a port of entry for the Beyond, for God coming into my life, indicating how close a bond there is between art and faith. Amos Wilder said once that God is a poet rather than a mathematician. God's dealing with the world, he said, is in the form of an epic poem, and our response is a psalm, a lyric, a doxology. Or, as Tom Driver puts it, we are forever trying to communicate the incommunicable, and this leads us inevitably to the symbolical and paradoxical language of poetry. In the introduction to his collection of *Poems of Doubt and Belief,* he writes:

> Religion is necessarily poetic and the validity of theology as an enterpise depends upon the viability of its understanding of poetry. . . . The dearest quality of poetry is that it catches us unawares and fills us with wonder. Perhaps

we are made to wonder that things are, that existence *is*. Perhaps we are taught suddenly that old things gain new life from new arrangement. . . . On the one side of metaphor (which is poetry's medium) lies science. On the other side lies a mystery that we sense to be unfathomable. Here are poems that move toward the boundaries of metaphor on the side of unfathomable mystery. So far the human spirit goes. Beyond, there is only the invocation and the unpredictable breath of the Spirit.[4]

Acknowledging the difficulties in giving a formal definition of poetry, our appreciation of it must depend largely not on what it *is* but on what it *does*. The poet John Ciardi says that we usually pose the wrong question about a poem. With furrowed brow we ask, "Now, what do you suppose this poem means?" Instead, he says, we should be asking, "*How* does this poem mean?" That is to say, the ways in which a poem handles a particular truth or insight, the flow of its language, and the images it invokes provide the best clues as to what it is all about. If all you are interested in is putting an idea into another person's head, you'll be wise to stick to no-nonsense prose. But poetry is more ambitious. Its intent is to get at parts of us that are hardest to reach. Take, for example, Randall Jarrell's brief poem, "The Death of the Ball Turret Gunner." These five lines of stark terror distill the tragedy reenacted thousands of times during World War II, all the sobbing, sickening grief and the obscenity of the plundering of young life. Official death lists tell only one part of the story. Jarrell's poem tells the other. Read it aloud; see *how* it means.

> From my mother's sleep I fell into the State,
> And I hunched in its belly till my wet fur froze.
> Six miles from earth, loosed from its dreams of life,
> I woke to black flak and the nightmare fighters.
> When I died they washed me out of the turret with a hose.[5]

It is only through such artistry that we can approach the problem of evil, let alone cope with it.

Poetry is both a private and a public exercise. It is pondering an experience you've had, distilling its essence, then telling others what it was like and how you feel about it. I've tried my hand at it, now and then. Take what I've called "Maine Blue Day."

> Sapphire-cut
> And set against the sun,
> This jeweled day is all awash
> With blue: azure and Alice,
> Wedgwood, robin's egg, and indigo.
>
> All else, except
> An emerald haze (for trees)
> Is white: thick bolts of Queen Anne's lace,
> Bluing-rinsed in surf;
> And gulls, a scream of feathers down the sky.
>
> Today is blue!
> Life, of course (to add
> A Teasdale touch) is multihued.
> I know that joy is gold,
> The brassy glint of trumpet tunes. I know
>
> That love is red;
> That pain is black, and peace
> A quiet, russet brown; that trouble's
> Mustard tan, and grace,
> Because it's always fresh, I'm sure is green,
>
> And April-new.
> But what I've learned today
> Here in this meadow, morning-washed,
> And tipping toward the sun,
> Is simply this: that hope is blue, to store
>
> Against the graying
> Years, the winter's cold,
> The heart's despair, November's dark.
> So, daisy-deep in June,
> A-sprawl beneath this blue, inverted cup,

> I'm newly wise, and quite content to lie
> And read my fortune in the brimming sky.

Poetry deals with the encroachments of the Beyond onto the human scene in its own special way. It keeps a door ajar, facilitating their entry. As a result, our sight is clearer, our vision enlarged. As someone has put it, poetry helps us to see; it helps us see what we see; and it helps us to see more than we see. It holds our journeys close to frontiers where high winds blow and the land drops off into mystery. But the experience is not limited to moments of ecstasy. The poetic can be found lurking in the most ordinary circumstances, on the most ordinary of days. Take, for instance, Richard Wilbur's poem "Love Calls Us to the Things of This World." Picture someone coming awake of a morning in an apartment (obviously before the day of washing machines and dryers!).

> The eyes open to a cry of pulleys,
> And spirited from sleep, the astounded soul
> Hangs for a moment bodiless and simple
> As false dawn.
>   Outside the open window
> The morning air is all awash with angels.
>
> Some are in bed-sheets, some are in blouses,
> Some are in smocks; but truly there they are.
> Now they are rising together in calm swells
> Of halcyon feeling, filling whatever they wear
> With the deep joy of their impersonal breathing;
>
> Now they are flying in space, conveying
> The terrible speed of their omnipresence, moving
> And staying like white water; and now of a sudden
> They swoon down into so rapt a quiet
> That nobody seems to be there.
>   The soul shrinks
>
> From all that it is about to remember,
> From the perpetual rape of every blessed day,

And cries,
"Oh, let there be nothing on earth but laundry,
Nothing but rosy hands in the rising steam
And clear dances done in the sight of heaven."

Yet, as the sun acknowledges
With a warm look the world's hunks and colors,
The soul descends once more in bitter love
To accept the waking body, and saying now
In a changed voice as the man yawns and rises,

"Bring them down from their ruddy gallows;
Let there be clean linen for the backs of thieves;
Let lovers go fresh and sweet to be undone,
And the heaviest nuns walk in a pure floating
Of dark habits,
          keeping their difficult balance.[6]

    Another way to illustrate the affinity between poetry and the "ordinary" is to cite instances in which the poetic, much to their surprise, emerges in the words and experiences of people who never for a moment suspected that they were in touch with it. It is my belief that lurking somewhere inside most of us there is a poet who needs to be coaxed into expression. Therefore, in leading groups of people interested in exploring the delight of poetry, I have made it a practice to invite them to write a poem. The usual response is vigorous demurral: "Write a poem? Who? Me! It's the last thing I could do!"

    I once extended this invitation to a group of ministers during a retreat I was conducting. One of them was especially vehement in his protest. I assured him it was only an invitation; he was free to accept or refuse. It was not an assignment. He thanked me and said he'd be playing golf with some of his friends that afternoon.

    When we reconvened for the evening session, I asked if there had been any poetic productivity, and if so, would anyone like to share what he or she had written. No response for a moment, and then it became clear that the golf-playing protester had something in his pocket. He allowed that he did but objected, not too strongly, to reading it. With the urging of his colleagues, he finally consented to do so, which he really wanted to do, anyway. "Refreshment" is scarcely a great lyric; it is clumsy and awkward in spots, but it is, essentially, a piece of writing that takes the poetic stance on an ordinary, everyday experience.

> I'm playing golf today.
> The sky is cloudless, sun, hot,
> No breeze.
> My mouth is cotton, straight from
> A medicine bottle.
>
> Ah—a pump I see!
> My clubs to the ground—I to the pump.
>
> A tin cup hangs on the pump!
> The years have not been kind to you,
> My friend. Ripped, battered, tarnished,
> Bent. Yet, I drink water
> From you—refreshment!
>
> The cup back to the hook, I pick up
> My clubs, and as I walk I begin to think:
> Ripped, battered, tarnished, bent, will I
> Be able to refresh?[7]

Here is "Tears," another by a nonpoet, a senior citizen member of another group I led.

> When nighttime came
> My eyes burned red and hot.
> At dawn they seemed
> Filled with grains of sand.
>
> So to my ophthalmologist I went
> Who examined them most carefully.
> "You are not producing
> Enough tears," he said.

"Take these three vials
And use them successively—
One drop in each eye
Six times a day.

In six weeks return
And let me know
Which one of these three
Give you the most relief."

The vial with the navy cap
Was labeled "Hypo-Tears,"
The lavender, "Liquifilm-Tears,"
The light blue one, "Tears Plus."

"Dear God, why is it
That I can shed
Only artificial tears
For a world threatened with extinction?"[8]

A radio broadcast engineer shared this with a group:

Everything dies in winter,
   My father did.
And I attended his interment on a raw, windblown day,
   Clouds coursing across a muted sun.
I stook there while words were said,
   Hand in coat pockets, hair awry,
A scene from a "B" movie.
Mourners acting, along for the ride.
We stood chilled by the event as much as by the day—
Forgetting that the frozen ground on which we stood
Still held the hope of Spring.[9]

Doggerel isn't really poetry, but the following sample, "Great Men and I," by an eleven-year-old boy has an essentially poetic stance to it.

Marconi made the wireless,
Pelito made the steeple,

> Lincoln fought for liberty
> To help the common people.
>
> Jim Thorpe was a football star,
> A patriot was Lee,
> Roosevelt was President,
> But I am only me.[10]

My favorite "junior" versifier, however, is a real poet. There is rich promise in these early efforts, written when she was nine or ten.

> Gazing into the vast expanse
> Of space, for stars, and, just by chance,
> To catch a glimpse of the world unknown,
> That scientific tests have shown,
>
> There's more to explore of space extensive:
> The universe is comprehensive.[11]

And here is "Civil Disobedience," a perfect example of a haiku—a Japanese verse form comprising seventeen syllables.

> Clear glass, when broken
> In the presence of light, casts
> A million rainbows.[12]

A seventeen-year-old high school girl sent me the following for pondering, and I've been doing just that ever since.

> more than once
>   I've missed a bus
>   but one day
> a chariot
>   came swinging low
>   even slow
> and I missed that
>   too.[13]

Again, poetry has its own way of getting at the truth, but it always has in mind, as with all genuine art, that its ultimate crtierion is just that—truth, not beauty. There is a tradition that tends to make us think just the opposite, namely, that whatever else it is, poetry must be beautiful; to be authentic, furthermore, it must deal with noble, elevating themes.

To be sure, a lot of great poetry is beautiful and ennobling. But it also explores ugliness and degradation. Were that not so, think what gaps there would be in our literary heritage: Greek tragedy, Shakespeare at his greatest in *Hamlet, Macbeth, Othello, King Lear!* Roger Hazelton is right in saying that in their honesty, artists often have unpleasant things to say and that these things cannot be said pleasantly. But they are often stated with such power and passion that they bring tears. What poets know better than other people is that in the search for truth it is necessary to pass through a wasteland. Albert Camus made that abundantly clear in his caution that very likely in order to find God, it becomes necessary to traverse that which denies God. Most of us can testify to that out of our own experiences: The road to spiritual maturity is not simply a gently spiraling path to heavenly heights. It often includes a detour through hell. In the same vein, long cherished practices and traditions are seen in a new and startling light once a poet has got hold of them. Watch what happens to a familiar, well-intentioned act of "charity" as Gwendolyn Brooks relates it in her poem "The Lovers of the Poor."

>   The Lovers of the Poor
>   arrive. The Ladies from the Ladies Betterment
> League
> Arrive in the late afternoon, . . .
> Walk in a gingerly manner up the hall. . . .
>   Their guild is giving money to the poor.
> The worthy poor. The very, very worthy
> And beautiful poor. Perhaps just not too swarthy?
> Perhaps just not too dirty nor too dim. . . .
>   But it's all so bad! and entirely too much for them.
> The stench; the urine, cabbage, and dead beans,
> Dead porridges of assorted dusty grains,

The old smoke, *heavy* diapers, and, they're told,
Something called chitterlings. . . .
               They've never seen such a make-do-ness as
Newspaper rugs before! In this, this "flat,"
Their hostess is gathering up the oozed, the rich
Rugs of the morning (tattered! the bespattered. . . .)
Readies to spread clean rugs for afternoon.
               Their League is allotting largess to the Lost.
But to put their clean, their pretty money, to put
Their money collected from delicate rose-fingers
Tipped with their hundred flawless rose-nails seems. . . .
               They own Spode, Lowestoft, candelabra,
Mantels and hostess gowns, and sunburst clocks,
Turtle soup, Chippendale, red satin "hangings,"
Aubussons and Hattie Carnegie. They winter
In Palm Beach; cross the Water in June; attend
When suitable, the nice Art Institute;
Buy the right books in the right binding. . . .
               Heavens! That
Was a rat, surely, off there, in the shadows? Long
And long-tailed? Gray? The Ladies from the Ladies'
Betterment League agree it will be better
To achieve the outer air that rights and steadies,
To hie to a house that does not holler, to ring
Bells elsetime, better presently to cater
To no more Possibilities, to get
Away. Perhaps the money can be posted. . . .
      Keeping their scented bodies in the center
Of the hall as they walk down the hysterical hall,
They allow their lovely skirts to graze no wall,
Are off at what they manage of a canter,
And resuming all the clues of what they were,
Try to avoid inhaling the laden air.[14]

All in all, the elusive mystery of poetry's power is expressed in these lines from Wallace Stevens's "The Man With the Blue Guitar."

> The man bent over his guitar,
> A shearsman of sorts. The day was green.
>
> They said, "You have a blue guitar,
> You do not play things as they are."
>
> The man replied, "Things as they are
> Are changed upon the blue guitar."
>
> And they said then, "But play, you must,
> A tune beyond us, yet ourselves,
>
> A tune upon the blue guitar
> Of things exactly as they are."[15]

A tune beyond me, but still *me!* It is the private, and public, secret of my survival. It is what has held me stubbornly to the discipline of using words correctly. For, if I have understood aright my vocation as a preacher and teacher, it has been to bring about an engagement between the gospel and the stuff of people's lives. Part of the job, of course, is to help them comprehend and manage ideas and concepts in good order. But there is far more to be done. Preachers and teachers are to be poets. As someone has expressed it, they are to enable people to discover "the poetic ambushed in the prosaic," to help them find hidden, unexpected meanings in coping with the ordinary, run-of-the-mill happenings of their daily lives, to listen with them for the sound of muted music and the rumble of distant thunder. Without that dimension in our communication skills, says the theologian Henri Nouwen, we may become simply manipulators of godly ideas.

Buechner sums it up when he indicates that if poetry, as one form of literature, is a metaphor for a writer's or a preacher's experience, it is at the same time a mirror in which we can see our own experiences reflected in a new and potentially transforming way. This, he says, is what it is like to search for God in a world where cruelty and pain hide God.

Laughter and God-Talk

From sly snicker to side-splitting convulsion, laughter is another port of entry into the life of the Spirit, a delightful way for the Holy to come in and have its way with me.

I relish a reported conversation between a young reporter and James Thurber. It was in an art gallery just prior to the opening of an exhibit of Thurber's drawings. When he stopped by to check on their hanging, the young man buttonholed him. "Mr. Thurber," he said, "I've long been one of your admirers, and now I have the chance to ask you a question." "Go right ahead," said Thurber. "What I'd like to know," said the reporter, "is how you characterize your work. For example, to what artistic school does it belong?" There was a pause. "What school?" said Thurber. "Frankly, I've never given the matter any attention, but now that you ask, I'd call it the 'Pre-Intentionalist.' That is to say, the ideas for most of my drawings occurred to me after I had drawn them."

It takes an airy, off-hand sitting loose like that to stay open to the invasions of the Beyond into our systematized, precisely engineered world. Its appearances cannot be forecast in the way we predict the arrival of Halley's comet. One of the clearest signs of grace is the element of surprise. I find people who laugh a lot to be among the most grace-full I know. They are not necessarily responding to something funny. With disarming frankness and an innate gaiety, they simply are indicating that they are very much at home in an open, unpredictable order of existence.

They refuse to be tethered to rigid formulas or confined to the requirements of a cult, conservative or liberal. They have an uncanny sense that at any moment carefully calculated plans may be upended, that what is fraudulent and pretentious may be exposed.

It is a melancholy fact, however, that for a long time our American Protestant tradition insisted that humor was a dubious ally of the sacred. Moral and spiritual matters were to be treated with appropriate solemnity, a seventeenth-century religious leader admonished. It is not proper, he said, to use games, sports, plays, or comedies among Christians. They do not agree, he said, with Christian silence, gravity, and sobriety. A hierarchy of emotions determined what was appropriate to times of worship and devotion. Laughter was outlawed, being considered frivolous, and thus out of keeping with the momentousness of faith.

We today have not yet been entirely freed from this oppressive point of view. Take those of us who are part of a so-called mainline congregation on a Sunday morning. On the whole, we are a fairly sober lot, although there has been considerable loosening up in more recent years, and I am grateful for it. After all, there are some inherently comical elements in the makeup of an average congregation, doubtful clerical humor aside. One is the very fact of our sitting there, taking ourselves so very seriously, often so very righteously, like the older brother in Jesus' parable, who was what Mark Twain once called "a good man in the worst sense of the word."

My Great Uncle William, I am afraid, was like that. His visits to our house, once a year on a Sunday in May, were a source of dread for me. It was not his formidable piety and awesome uprightness as much as it was a small incident that marked his visit year after year.

Uncle William arrived in midafternoon, coming out from Brooklyn on the "Rapid." We gathered in the sitting room, and listened respectfully to his expansive commentary on matters moral and spiritual, mostly from a conservative, Presbyterian stance. Right on schedule, at five o'clock, grandmother would extend a cordial invitation to supper—just "pot luck," no fuss—although I knew very well that the menu had been carefully planned. Invariably, Uncle William would demur, saying he had to get back to Brooklyn. Grandmother pressed with discreet urgency, and finally the old gentleman yielded over a continuing murmur of protests. We sat down at table, Grandmother asked our guest to say grace, and quiet panic seized me. "The moment" was at hand. Uncle William launched into his address to the Almighty, in which, with encyclopedic thoroughness, he expressed gratitude for every conceivable mercy, including a number that I could not recognize. Finally, he came to the point of petitioning the Lord that the food we were about to eat "might strengthen our weak and frail bodies." It was a moment of sheer agony, for opposite me at the table was my older brother, a mountain of a man (he was twelve years older than I) ruddy-faced, and bursting with good health and vitality. As best I could, but with small success, I tried to choke back, swallow, do anything I could to suppress the laughter strangling in my throat. Fortunately, Uncle William drew to a close shortly thereafter, and upon his "Amen," Grandmother swiftly urged us to get on with the meal, lest "the vittles get cold."

Actually there was a lot that was downright funny about those early years in the family, in spite of its shaky foundations. Much of it was tied to the belated move by our household into the twentieth century in terms of "modern improvements." We were, I am sure, the last in the neighborhood to catch up.

The first advance was in illumination, from kerosene lamps to electricity. (I took a special delight in it, for one of my weekly chores was to clean, refill, and trim the lamps.) The day arrived when electric installation was complete and the power was to be turned on. Grandmother, who was blessed with a certain native sense of the dramatic, arranged a brief ceremonial to celebrate the occasion. In the early evening, we gathered in the dining room, chosen because it boasted the largest and most elaborate fixture. It hung over the table, a large, inverted china bowl surrounded by four bell-like china pendants. At a prearranged signal, Grandmother pushed the black button (with its mother-of-pearl center), and accompanied by cries of "modified rapture," a great glory flooded the room. It was quickly established, however, that for everyday lighting, use of the whole fixture was unthinkably extravagant, and one sixty-watt bulb in one of the china bells would suffice. An exception was made, however. Sunday evening supper, which had a certain elegance about it (whether Uncle William was with us or not), was appointed as the time for special indulgence in household lighting. Hence, part way through the meal, I was accorded the privilege of climbing on my chair, reaching inside the china bowl, and turning on its own sixty-watt bulb! How the silverware and china gleamed in the suffused glow! And how wickedly expensive!

Next came the telephone, a two-party line. No nonsense here, either. Its use was to be strictly utilitarian, for necessary business or household-maintenance calls; for personal calls only of an urgent nature; no idle chitchatting. Moreover, the telephone was put at the foot of the stairs, the most public as well as, in the winter, the coldest place in the house (only three of the downstairs rooms being heated).

After a decent interval, we moved to the miracle of radio, a crystal set, with one pair of earphones. This limited facility held to a minimum the questionable enjoyment of such pagan entertainment as Jones and Hare, "The Happiness Boys," or the nightly adventures of "Amos and Andy."

The most radical step in the march of progress at 38 Merrick Road was the installation of a "closet bowl," as it was delicately referred to. One of the uncles vigorously protested it as sheer indulgence, as one more piece of evidence of the softness that was overtaking American society. In recognition of his scruples, the weather-beaten outdoor facility was left standing. Again with her dramatic flair, Grandmother staged a brief ceremonial of dedication. It was after school, in the afternoon. While I waited in the hall, the female members of the household retired into the bathroom. There was a long pause, followed by the sound of a mighty, rushing stream, much giggling, and the pronouncement of general availability!

Happily, we have moved toward a more holistic understanding of ourselves, whatever situation we may be in, including worship. Laughter is so much a part of us that there never can be a question about coming into God's presence with all parts accounted for. We should never be obligated to leave an authentic piece of us to cool its heels in the vestibule of faith while the rest of us enters a fumigated holy of holies.

Needless to say, humor is a highly subjective matter. The human funny bone comes in a wide variety of shapes and sizes. I'll never understand—and there is no reason why I should—why so many people find Steve Martin, for example, absolutely convulsing. Or why, for me, Jonathan Winters is one of the funniest people alive, while Johnny Carson can scarcely induce a smile. Victor Borge never fails to delight, and Joan Rivers sends me into a mild depression. For me, the lunacy of the Marx brothers (for example, their demolition of a performance of *Il Trovatore* at the Metropolitan Opera House) is the ultimate in soul-deep laughter; for some of my friends, it is a mindless display of bad taste.

The subjective aspect of humor affords, in a way, an insight into the uniqueness of each of us as an individual, the particular way we have of responding to the mysterious. Take the jokes we tell or the cartoons that make us laugh. They are more self-revealing, I suspect, than we realize. Take the cartoon of a man riding a New York subway train at rush hour, as I had to do frequently at one period in my life. (And if you have never had that experience, you can't really appreciate what's funny.) A couple of pigeons are perched on the man's shoulder. He shrugs off the understandable curiosity of his fellow passengers who are staring at him, saying, "Don't ask me; they got on at Fifty-ninth Street!" Or consider a cartoon picturing one of the great dams of the West. Down at its base, a beaver is explaining things to a puzzled rabbit. "I didn't actually build it," says the beaver, "but it was based on my idea."

Let it be said, also, that there is a kind of laughter that cannot be honored. It is the laughter of sheer ridicule, degrading the dignity of another human being; laughter at physical or mental disabilities or at someone's misfortune.

The comic, therefore, requires an element of the sacredness of life, but at the same time, it reminds us that the sacred requires a healthy, running comment of the comic. Laughter without faith may lead to cynicism, but faith without laughter ends up in lifeless, pedantic dogmatism. The playfulness of humor, spontaneous eruptions of laughter are as much legitimate responses to the sacred as is grave solemnity. A religion without an innate gaiety and a propensity to laughter about it is a defective vessel for conveying divine truth.

What are the uses of laughter? It is, in one sense, an absurd and inappropriate question, for there is a fundamental aspect to laughter that disavows any utilitarian function. With our moralistic bent, we are forever looking for ways to legitimize a thing in terms of how *useful* it can be. To do so, implies a basic misunderstanding of what laughter is, essentially. Like a number of other things, laughter is something you *do*, not talk about (as I am doing now, which, of course, is laughable!). It is not, like the sombre, brow-wrinkling essay by a noted theologian I once read, discussing the relationship between humor and faith. Laughter does not require a peg of reason on which to hang a justification for itself. There need not be any more rationale behind it than the experience of laughing itself. I remember the once famous "laughing record" we used to play on our phonograph (in its day one of the marvels of technology). It began with the uncertain squeak of a violin, obviously in the hands of a rank amateur. After the third or fourth sour note, there was a titter in the audience. More, louder titters, then a few unsuppressed giggles, and, before long, a mounting crescendo of laughter reaching an uncontrolled pitch of delirium, in which we, of course, by that time, were helplessly involved.

A lot of laughter in my family is like that. It happens most often among a certain quartet. Almost anything—or nothing—can trigger it. Once started, it spreads as uncontrolled contagion from one to another. And, should a sobersides rationalist on the sidelines ask what, please, might be the reason for such unbounded hilarity, a fresh outburst is the only response. Thoreau said that we need "the tonic of wildness," in order to stay fully human. Just so do we need the tonic of madness, the laughter, for instance, of pure farce, where normal situations are reduced to chaos, where logic is dismantled and lunacy takes over.

Again, laughter serves to keep us in our place, as people, that is. We need it in order to be kept aware of our earthenware humanity, to keep us from taking ourselves and our ambitions too seriously, our strained, self-righteous efforts to be "good," for example. One of Thurber's fables, "The Seal Who Became Famous," is to the point.

> A seal who lay basking on a large, smooth rock said to himself, "All I ever do is swim. None of the other seals can swim any better than I can," he reflected, "but, on the other hand, they can swim just as well." The more he pondered the monotony and uniformity of his life, the more depressed he became. That night he swam away and joined a circus.
>
> Within two years the seal had become a great balancer. He could balance lamps, billiard cues, medicine balls, hassocks, taborets, dollar cigars, and anything else you gave him. When he read in a book a reference to the Great Seal of the United States, he thought it meant him. In the winter of his third year as a performer he went back to the large, smooth rock to visit his friends and family. He gave them the Big Town stuff right away: the latest slang, liquor in a golden flask, zippers, a gardenia in his lapel. He balanced for them everything there was on the rock to balance, which wasn't much. When he had run through his repertory, he asked the other seals if they could do what he had done, and they all said no. "O.K.," he said, "Let's see you do something I can't do." Since the only

thing they could do was swim, they all plunged off the rocks into the sea. The circus seal plunged right after them, but he was so hampered by his smart city clothes, including a pair of seventeen dollar shoes, that he began to founder at once. Since he hadn't been in swimming for three years, he had forgotten what to do with his flippers and tail, and he went down for the third time before the other seals could reach him. They gave him a simple but dignified funeral.

Moral: Whom God has equipped with flippers should not monkey around with zippers.[16]

Laughter is why clowns and mimes of all kinds are able to comment eloquently on the human scene. In their modest way, in sharp contrast to the brittle gloss and frenetic pace of so many stand-up comedians, they gently mirror our eccentricities and the bloated estimates we make of ourselves. Their pratfalls and extravagant gestures expose our absurd claims of self-importance. Their wordless acting out of scenarios quite familiar to us is a loving signal that a fresh look at our behavior and attitudes is called for. They remind us that we are constantly under a scrutiny that never lets us out of its sight. Isabella, in *Measure for Measure*, puts her finger on it.

> Man, proud man,
> Dressed in a little brief authority,
> Most ignorant of what he's most assured,
> His glassy essence, like an angry ape,
> Plays such fantastic tricks before high heaven
> As make the angels weep.[17]

Clearly, it must be acknowledged that laughter has a useful role. It has healing powers. Norman Cousins has documented this in *Anatomy of an Illness*. He tells how with the help of doctors and nurses, a program was developed calling for the exercise of the affirmative emotions as a factor in enhancing bodily chemistry.

It was easy enough to have hope, and love, and faith, but what about laughter? Nothing is less funny than being flat on your back with all the bones in your spine and joints hurting. A systematic program was indicated. A good place to begin, I thought, was with amusing movies. Allen Funt, producer of the spoofing television program "Candid Camera," sent films of some of his CC classics, along with a motion picture projector. The nurse was instructed in its use. We were even able to get our hands on some old Marx Brothers films. We pulled down the blinds and turned on the machine.

It worked. I made the joyous discovery that ten minutes of genuine belly laughter had an anesthetic effect and would give me at least two hours of pain-free sleep. When the pain-killing effect of the laughter wore off, we would switch on the motion picture projector again, and, not infrequently, it would lead to another pain-free interval . . . .

How scientific was it to believe that laughter—as well as the positive emotions in general—was affecting my body chemistry for the better? If laughter did in fact have a salutory effect on the body's chemistry, it seemed at least theoretically likely that it would enhance the system's ability to fight the inflammation. So we took sedimentation rate readings just before, as well as several hours after, the laughter episodes. Each time there was a drop of at least five points. The drop itself was not substantial, but it held and was cumulative. I was greatly elated by the discovery that there is a physiologic basis for the ancient theory that laughter is good medicine.[18]

Finally, laughter, too, is a means of grace, I've discovered. There are theological dimensions involved, which is to say that laughter is one form of God-talk.

Actually, there isn't very much in the Bible that strikes us as funny, at least not in the sense we tend to use the word—things like jokes, comic stories, one-liners. There is, of course, the often cited and priceless story in the Book of

Genesis of Abraham getting the word from the Lord that at the ripe old age of ninety, Sarah was going to have a baby. She was behind the door, eavesdropping, and got the giggles. When the Lord asked her why she was laughing, a piece of the Puritan in her prompted her denial. "Oh yes," said the Lord, "you *did* laugh," and apparently was pleased by it, for the expectant parents were informed that the baby's name was to be Isaac, which, in Hebrew, means laughter!

The laughter of Christian faith is, essentially, a response to incongruity, to wild, impossible things that actually happen. That God should single out a little-known, singularly stiff-necked tribe of Semites as a "Chosen People" and expect them to be the bearers and agents of divine purpose strikes one as an absurdity and is good for a laugh. Then, that God, Creator of the universe, the One who comprehends the incomprehensible reaches of interstellar space, should choose to enter the earthly scene as a human being, on the face of it, sounds incongruous. And that's not all. The details of the whole preposterous arrangement strain our credulity still further: entry on the scene in a smelly cow barn behind the local pub of an obscure up-country town; a carpenter's family, fishing folk, neighbors with shadowy reputations. And, most unbelievable of all, the sheer degradation of death by crucifixion! All of it in the name of a divine, eternal purpose!

The fact is that it all happened; it has God's stamp and seal. And if we laugh at it, it is our mirth at a basic incongruity in existence: that the infinite is involved in the finite, that God and human affairs are inextricably mixed. It is what the apostle Paul called "the foolishness of the Gospel." And, said Paul, the foolishness of God is wiser than the best wisdom of men and women! Now and then, the Beyond breaks through the insulation of contemporary culture wrapped so tightly around our lives—sometimes in darkness and suffering, and sometimes in peals of laughter.

Peter DeVries, one of the best novelists of our time,

makes a convincing case for what he calls "comic seriousness:" that laughter is a way to view life; that closer to anything than laughter are our tears. Comedy and tragedy are tangled in the same web of experience. Agreeing with W.H. Auden, he believes that only through comedy can we be serious. He has written some twenty novels, all in the comic mode. He pokes fun at the human scene, pricks all kinds of pretentious bubbles, especially those of suburbia. There is *Reuben, Reuben, Let Me Count the Ways, Through the Fields of Clover, Into Your Tent I'll Creep, Madder Music.* But in *The Blood of the Lamb* his writing makes a wide turn. His wit is as sharp as ever, but then he reaches into deep places of personal tragedy—the death of his young daughter at the end of a long battle with leukemia. In the novel (his own story), he becomes Don Wanderhope on a desperate search for meaning, having somehow survived a series of crippling events—his own savage illness, the death of a brother, a tortured marriage and divorce, and, finally, Carol's pitiable, agonizing illness.

There is an unforgettable scene at the end of the novel. Don has gone to the hospital. It is Carol's twelfth birthday, and he has brought a cake to celebrate it with her. But on arrival, he learns that she has died. He leaves the hospital, carrying the now useless cake. Stumbling along the street, he comes to St. Catherine's Church, which he and Carol had often passed and where he had spent hours trying to patch together a few shreds of meaning for his tattered life. He pauses at the front steps and looks up at the familiar figure of the crucified Christ over the entrance. Suddenly, he says, he was engulfed by grief and a flood of memories—of the child's gallantry during her illness, and of her great gift of humor. He thinks of the countless times they gave way to uncontrolled laughter and especially of the enthusiasm they shared for old silent comedies with their custard pie-throwing scenes. It was one of their private jokes.

All at once he is seized with an irrepressible impulse. He balances the birthday cake on the palm of his hand, draws back and lets fly with all his strength.

Before the mind snaps or the heart breaks, it gathers itself like a clock about to strike. . . . It was miracle enough that the pastry should reach its target at all. . . . The more so that it should land squarely, just beneath the crown of thorns. Then through scalded eyes I seemed to see the hands free themselves of the nails and move slowly toward the soiled face. Very slowly, very deliberately, with infinite patience, the icing was wiped from the eyes and flung away. . . . Then the cheeks were wiped down with the same sense of gentle ritual, with all the kind sobriety of one whose voice could be heard saying, "Suffer the little children to come unto me, for of such is the kingdom of heaven.". . . Then the scene dissolved itself in a mist in which my legs could no longer support their weight, and I sank down to the steps. . . Thus [I] was found at that place said to be the only alternative to the muzzle of a pistol: the foot of the cross.[19]

So, in a curious way, laughter is much of what it is all about—deep, throaty laughter at a divine joke, God's joke, as Beuchner calls it. It is the outlandishness of God who does impossible things with impossible people—even the likes of me! It is the laughter that rises when we realize how often God's grace comes to us in small, insignificant, even absurd ways. And back of it all, there rings a kind of cosmic hilarity, the laughter of One who derides and condemns the evil and violence of people and nations and whose vision of a world of justice and peace is never dimmed by our faithlessness and defections. It is there in the second psalm, and it is there that we put our trust: "Why do the nations conspire and the peoples plot in vain? The kings of the earth set themselves, and the rulers take counsel together. . . . [The Lord] who sits in the heavens laughs."

Sound of the Beyond

Any attempt to illuminate with words an experience that is essentially wordless ends in frustration. Poetry goes further than anything else, but it, too, has its limits. In the end, all forms of nonverbal communication have to rely on the special magic of their own medium, like music for example. There is no way to make very clear to another person just what a movement of a symphony means and does to you, short of having the same sounds resonate in that person's ears and heart in the same way they do in yours. Even when there is an especially good wedding of text and music, it is the melody, the rhythms, the cadences of the music that make the difference.

Even so, for all the frustration, such limitation serves to emphasize the power of the nonverbal to communicate what syntax and grammar simply cannot handle—the ineffable, the other-worldly, the mysterious. Their kinds of truth rely largely on intimation and, often, only oblique, fugitive references. Moreover, when we are stirred by great music, we are reminded of the provincialism of our humanity and that there are galaxies of beauty and meaning millions of sound years away. Now and then, we are privileged to hear an echo of them, to snatch a fragment of song that no words of ours, however learned or polished, could possibly describe. With Shakespeare's poetry straining at its limits, this is what Lorenzo is trying to explain to Jessica in the magical moonlit scene in *The Merchant of Venice:*

> How sweet the moonlight sleeps upon this bank!
> Here we will sit and let the sound of music
> Creep in our ears; soft stillness and the night
> Become the touches of sweet harmony.
> Sit, Jessica. Look how the floor of heaven
> Is thick inlaid with patines of bright gold:
> There's not the smallest orb which thou behold'st
> But in his motion like an angel sings,
> Still quiring to the young-eyed cherubins.
> Such harmony is in immortal souls;
> But whilst this muddy vesture of decay
> Doth grossly close it in, we cannot hear it.[20]

But now and then, by a special grace, we *do* hear it, a sound so exquisite that we are moved to tears, to ecstasy, to claim a new truth, or, in Rilke's phrase, to change our lives!

As with humor, of course, whatever opens the gates to another world is a highly subjective matter. Music that speaks eloquently to one person may turn another off completely. My musical tastes, I confess, lie across a relatively short spectrum; they are marked by highly personal prejudices. Except for the great choral works of Bach, notably the *B Minor Mass* and the *Passion According to St. Matthew*, by and large, baroque music does not stir my blood. Its elegance and formal structure reach my head but seldom my heart. I have the same reaction to much contemporary music. I know that jazz is an authentic American art form, one of the few "originals" in our culture, but I find it hard to listen to. My chief delight is in the world of musical theater—the operas of Rossini, Donizetti, Bellini, Verdi, Wagner, and Puccini, and, in lighter vein, the classic operettas of Strauss, Lehar, and Kalman, and the comic, satirical masterpieces of Gilbert and Sullivan.

Over the years, music has been for me one of the most precious gifts of the Beyond to my life. It has spoken to my heart when sage advice has been exhausted, when there have been no words left to ease pain or comfort sorrow. It has afforded a private sanctuary when all I needed was to be alone. Often I have marveled how a particular succession of notes fashioned into a melody, beating to a particular rhythm, has had the power to pull me up short, stop me dead in my tracks, and turn me about. It's what happens to me, for example, when I hear the slow movement of Beethoven's Ninth Symphony, the simple purity of "The Ash Grove," the Welsh hymn tune "Rhosymedre," or the matchless mix of words and tune of "Drink to Me Only With Thine Eyes."

There is music that for me makes clear that part of the bedrock of existence is an irrepressible joy. There is the infectious lilt of Strauss's operetta *Die Fledermaus*. There is the final scene of Verdi's *Falstaff*. It was his last opera and his final commentary on the human venture. After a lifetime of composing very "grand" operas with their tales of murder, revenge, and the darkest of tragedies, he turned to Shakespeare's merriest of comedies for his valedictory.

There is music that reaches the bleakest of my experiences, the shadowed places through which I have had to walk. One of the great moments in music distills it into an essence. It is the experience of desolation, of someone knowing the anguish of abandonment. It is Verdi, again, there in the last act of *Otello*. Desdemona is fatally caught in the trap of Otello's rage, induced by his irrational conviction that she has been unfaithful to him. Unable to convince him of her innocence, at his orders she has retired to her chamber. To an eerie woodwind accompaniment, she sings a plaintive ballad her mother taught her about a girl who was abandoned by her lover. Then in the flickering lamplight, she kneels and against the moaning of the night winds sings the "Ave Maria." She climbs into bed. All that is left is darkness and the muted muttering of the lowest strings in the orchestra. There is a slight sound, and the shadowy figure of Otello is at the door.

There is music and the crucifixion. I have read the record of it countless times, especially in the fifteenth chapter of the Gospel of Mark. But because music can convey the agony of it more powerfully than even those words, on Good Friday I set aside time to be alone to listen to a recording of the "Crucifixus" of Bach's *B Minor Mass*. Note by note, it spells out the tragic scene, a sobbing treble over a reiterated bass theme, the volume steadily diminishing, measure by measure, until the broken body is laid in the sepulcher, and the music dies away in a barely audible whisper.

There is music to mark the achievement of quiet acceptance: of life's inevitable changes, of new limitations, of putting the past in its place and facing tomorrow with inner serenity, I listen to it with special appreciation, here in these lengthening years. It is Hans Sachs of Wagner's *Die Meistersinger*, under his linden tree in the magic of a midsummer evening, coming to terms with himself and the passing of time, the mellow horns of the orchestra reflecting the breadth and warmth of his spirit.

It's Thoreau's salted wisdom all over again—the importance of stepping to the music we hear with our inner ear!

Snow Peaks and the Holy

Things came to a head, so to speak, in the late fall. I had run out of time, and the family out of patience. It had to do with my long fascination (shall I say obsession) with the Himalayas. They hadn't any objection to it; they simply were tired of hearing about a "some-day" trip to see them. I had retired from full-time ministry, allowing opportunity for such a venture, but I felt I could not, or more accurately *should* not, plan such a trip. For one thing, it was too expensive. For another, I should have to go without Eleonore, who was working full-time, and that would border on the sinful, since all our major undertakings had been joint enterprises. Besides, the whole proposition smacked of sheer self-indulgence, and this distressed the Puritan I had not yet dislodged from my aging back.

The family moved in on me, gently, lovingly, saying in effect: "Look, we're really happy about your enthusiasm for the Himalayas and a trip to Nepal, but what we want to know is: are you, or aren't you, going to take it? If you are, get with it; if you aren't, dear father, dear husband, we have to tell you that we are getting a little tired of hearing about it!" Taking that to be more than just a mild suggestion, I headed for a travel agency the next day. Not only that, with the gusty winds of newborn freedom still blowing, I signed up, not only for three weeks in Nepal but for six days in Vienna, with an expensive seat at the opera every night! Came Christmas shortly thereafter and a gift for me from the family: seed money for the enterprise in an envelope marked "Nepal Relief Fund."

Fascination with the Himalayas had set in early. I first got hooked by reading the accounts of the early British expeditions, especially the valorous, but unsuccessful attempts to reach the summit of Everest, the world's highest peak. Later, with the opening of Nepal to the rest of the world, expeditions were resumed, and I became an armchair member of most of them. One after another, the great peaks were climbed: Everest, Lhotse, Kangchenjunga, K2, Annapurna, Dhaulagiri, Nanga Parbat, Manaslu, Nuptse, Shishapangma. The geography of Nepal became as familiar as that of Massachusetts. And always looming over the pages of my book were those 1,500 miles of icy ramparts thrusting 28,000 feet and more into the northern sky—"the snows" of the world's greatest mountain range. Their geology has been carefully studied. All kinds of scientific data about them have been assembled and analyzed: weather conditions, wind velocities, violent storms, the effects of high altitudes on the human body and mind. But for all the amassed information about them, they are still among the vast unknown quantities of the planet. They soar into the thin air of the borderland between Nepal and Tibet but also into the region where all our knowledge, testing and measuring, and technological expertise peter out, and mystery takes over. I spent three weeks in uninterrupted veneration of their awesome beauty, hiking trails or sprawled in a chair on the lawn of the small hotel in Pokhara, a trade route junction in central Nepal. From there, at an elevation of 3,500 feet, I looked across 25 miles of foothills to the Annapurna massif, one of the earth's most dazzling showpieces, more than 26,000 feet high!

The peaks riveted attention through all the shifting patterns of light and shade during the daylight hours, but at sunrise, and again at sunset, they glowed for a few moments with the indescribable glory of another world beyond the rim of this fretful habitation. Each morning, before daybreak, I went up to the flat roof of the hotel and settled in a spot affording a full view of the forthcoming spectacle. Except for the dull glint of starlight, land and sky were shrouded in predawn blackness. The only sounds were the quiet murmur of the voices of others gathered to wait and to watch. In a few minutes it began. First, a barely discernible gray-white blur a short distance above the northern horizon, while off to the east, the sky took on a faint glow. Before long, the gray-white patch turned to pale pink, then to a deeper hue, then to a molten rose-gold, steadily growing in intensity and washing down the southern flank of Annapurna. The sun was still minutes below the horizon, the valley still a murky black. But, already, high above us, on a schedule set by a timing far beyond our own, a new day sprang fresh and gleaming from the hand of God.

I have pondered this fascination of mine with mountains. Perhaps I am simply a romantic pantheist at heart. (I can surmise sadder possibilities.) But it goes deeper than that. Like poetry, like music, mountains are part of that frontier where astonishing, scalp-tingling things happen, where I am reminded of an ultimate mystery against which, choose it or not, my little life is set, and where I am cleansed and renewed in the presence of a pure, unalloyed beauty.

As has often been reported, George Mallory, one of the great figures in the history of mountaineering, on setting out for another attempt on Everest, was asked: "Why do you keep trying to climb this mountain?" He replied: "Because it is there." It is a simple, not particularly profound answer, but perhaps the best that can be given. It would be my reply, too, but for a different reason. Mallory spoke as a climber. To reach a summit was the response to a challenge. It was a test of human proficiency, a way to measure one's stockpile of strength against primal forces of nature. James Ullman, in his book *The Age of Mountaineering*, tells about one of the climbers on the north face of Everest who realizes that he has reached his limit and that he must turn back. Before starting down, he fixes his eyes on the summit and says, "Just wait, old thing, we'll get you yet!"

But, the gallant record of modern mountaineering notwithstanding, mountains do not exist to be climbed, to be conquered, to be "got." They are more than just a proving ground for human endurance and skills. Mallory was right: They are simply "there." Reaching their summits, or hiking on their lower slopes, or even just standing in their awesome presence, we remember more clearly who we are—creatures designed by the hand of God, possessing unbelievable potential but also subject to crippling handicaps and aware of how fragile our lives really are. At any rate, for me high mountains are more a means of assessing the elemental aspects of my humanity than of measuring physical prowess or my powers of endurance. And, whatever else, they are a constant reminder of how close I live to the borders of the Unknown.

Moreover, I've learned from my interest in mountaineering that there is nothing softheaded or sentimental about it. It is a demanding, disciplined pursuit, and its devotees are always at the edge of danger. This has led me to reexamine a metaphor we commonly use in describing a particular religious event. How often we have heard people, at a summer conference, let's say, tell about worshiping at vespers at sunset on a hillside, listening to a charismatic leader talk about spirituality, or being nourished by a special kind of fellowship, and summing it all up with the words "a mountaintop experience." Likely as not, at the closing service they were enjoined to leave the mountain and descend to the grubby valleys of the world, where, freshly inspired, they would become more diligent in combating injustice and prejudice, more Christ-like in behavior. It's not a matter of putting down anybody's testimony to a valid spiritual experience, but it might be instructive to put next to it the account of some of the great ascents of history and to note a marked difference in circumstances. For example, there was Moses' climb up Mount Sinai, his hair-raising encounter with the Almighty on the summit, and his descent, which ended in a burst of furious anger toward the people God had called him to serve! There was the mountaintop transfiguration experience. When the disciples who had gone with Jesus to the top of the mountain saw what was happening to him, they were scared to death and simply could not handle it.

Nor does the literature of modern mountaineering describe what happened on most summit efforts as particularly exalting or spirit-filled. Instead, what is generally reported is a grueling test of endurance under subhuman conditions, crouching on a knife-edge of rock in thirty-degrees-below-zero weather, in the teeth of a gale blowing at eighty miles an hour. And the descent, more than once, sheer horror, like that of the first expedition to the summit of Annapurna.

People go to the mountains, said Ullman once, because they need the mountains, because they find behind the ranges things that are hidden from them in the life of the plains. It has been that way with me. The metaphor of mountains, as a sign of spiritual meaning and power, has dominated the skyline of my years. As with Jerusalem, there have always been mountains around my life. There is a kind of holiness for me in acknowledging that simple truth.

"A Little Touch of Harry in the Night"

One of the unforgettable moments in Shakespeare comes in *King Henry V*, in the prologue to Act IV. The Chorus sets the scene of the English camp the night before the fateful battle of Agincourt. The young king is moving among his anxious troops, going from campfire to campfire rallying their spirits.

> Who will behold
> The royal captain of this ruin'd band
> Walking from watch to watch, from tent to tent,
> Let him cry "Praise and glory on his head!"
> For forth he goes and visits all his host;
> Bids them good morrow with a modest smile,
> And calls from brothers, friends, and countrymen.
> Upon his royal face there is no note
> How dread an army hath enrounded him. . . .
> That every wretch, pining and pale before,

> Beholding him, plucks comfort from his looks:
> A largesse universal, like the sun,
> His liberal eye doth give to every one,
> Thawing cold fear. Then mean and gentle all,
> Behold, as may unworthiness define, a little
> Touch of Harry in the night.[21]

There are times, to be sure, when, to stay alive, we have to be alone, guarding our private terrain from intrusion, preserving "the silence within," and I shall speak more of this later. But, we are also born to be companions, to share our lives with those who care, gratefully accepting the discipline of mutual accountability. It is to sense, above all, "the throb of compassion," as DeVries expresses it. It is "the recognition of how long, how long is the mourners' bench upon which we sit, arms linked in undeluded friendship, all of us, brief links, ourselves, in the eternal pity." It is grasping an elemental truth about us—that we are never completely alone, that there is a caring that hangs on through the deepest darkness, waiting with an infinite patience to come light again. It is caring, incarnate, acted out by another person who recognizes and honors our need. It is my experience that the most authentic sign of grace is to sense in my season of aloneness "a little touch of Harry in the night," or of Tom, Ruth, Jerry, Mr. B., or queer old Mrs. Quinn.

Theologically speaking, it's what we mean by Incarnation—love taking human shape, a breakthrough of the Beyond into our lives bringing healing and hope, pulsing with "the throb of compassion."

My experiences of it have varied in form and style. There is, first, the influence on my life of certain grace-full people. Some of them are close friends; some I have known only slightly; others have spoken to me through their writing and teaching. But, remembering Charles Péguy's comment about grace coming to us sometimes from the circumference as well as from the center, I name them in gratitude, instances of intrusions of the Holy, even if only in bits and pieces.

There are those who helped me hone my skills as a communicator. Chief among them was Harry Emerson Fosdick. We were not personal friends, but in his classes at seminary, I got my head and my heart straight about preaching: that it is both a disciplined craft to be worked at, in season and out, and an exercise in human relationships demanding exquisite sensitivity to the plights of people. I learned from him that if a sermon is to reach into the deep places of another person's life as an announcement of good news, it first has to pass through the filter of one's own personal encounter with it, free of pussyfooting, or cant, or "pious blah," as he once bluntly described the homiletical effort of a student in his class.

There are others who modeled forms and styles of ministry for me: Samuel Miller and Frederick Buechner, for example, with their dogged insistence that words are nothing less than a sacrament and that the way something is said largely determines whether or not it will get a hearing. There was Paul Scherer, too, who taught me, as I've said earlier, that a poetic stance is imperative for truth telling.

Again, as I have noted earlier, there are the novelists, playwrights, and poets, many of them "secular," as we think of them, who have illuminated the Holy for me in memorable ways.

There are those who have weathered the storms that devastate our interior landscapes from time to time and who have emerged with a new dignity and serenity of spirit. There is my friend Chris, who at the bottom of alcoholism and depression, with the help of Alcoholics Anonymous and a prayer group at his church, "came to himself" and rejoined society, exactly the kind of "new life" experience the New Testament talks about from start to finish.

There are glints and snatches of the Holy for me in the purity and single-mindedness of people who spend themselves in commitment to a commanding cause. Like Mary, well into her senior years. She works untiringly, with an undiscourageable hope, at the business of achieving a world at peace, rid of nuclear arms, speaking, writing, pleading, demonstrating, making it very clear which side shall know "the stubborn ounces" of her weight!

I have been aware of the presence of the Holy at those times of crisis and testing when another person came to stand beside me. Again Henry Sloan Coffin's phrase: "No substitute for personal presence." There was Frank. He learned of my resignation from the New England church where tension was mounting and I was persuaded that continuing damage would be the result of my staying on. Within hours, he put in a long-distance call to express his love and concern and to tell me about a ministry in which I might be interested. And there was Bob, just out of seminary, living in a distant part of the country and on the minimal salary of his first charge. He learned of our son Joe's death and promptly boarded a plane to be with us for the memorial service.

There have been others who stood by during the difficult days of the deterioration of my family situation and my break with it, the minister of our church, for instance. He was a genial, burly Irishman, keenly aware of my aborted efforts to bring about some kind of reconciliation. He told me he thought I had done all I could under the circumstances and that I did not have to demean myself in the face of intransigence.

Similarly, there were other veterans of ministry who shared their seasoned wisdom, who gave wise counsel and support in the early days of my ministry when I found it hard to tell which side was up and which was down. There was Frederick Stamm, who made a heavy, and risky, investment of trust in my limited talents when I became his assistant in a Brooklyn church.

I am grateful, too, for a whole succession of "support" groups of one kind or another over the years. It began with a small company of us hard at work in ecumenical youth activities in New York City. There was the monthly gathering of ministers and spouses with a "no holds barred" approach to one another and to the exasperations and satisfactions of ministry. Later came life-sharing "Shalom" groups, outgrowths of human relations laboratories and exercises in sensitivity training spawned by the human potential movement, to which I am heavily indebted for invaluable help in moving toward the full ownership and self-management of my life. Over the years, Eleonore and I have been the beneficiaries of such little companies of caring people, bonded in a covenant of openness, honesty, and trust. Here in our retirement community, we continue to be nourished week after week by such a group.

Without nurturing relationships such as these, I know that I should not have come very far. But were it not for the incredible trust and caring of my family, I probably would not have made it at all! By "family" I mean, of course, those who are of my own flesh. But I mean more than that; I mean an "extended" family, those who are part of an intimate circle, not by blood but by a covenant of caring. Because of what we know about one another, because of what we have suffered and rejoiced over together, because of what we have given to and received from one another, our relationship has taken on the properties of a sacrament. Our bond is an unconditional love that has "happened" between us, not conditioned by ties of lineage or loyalties of kinship but by marrow-deep recognition of something inviolate and unchanging.

> Love is not love
> Which alters when it alteration finds,
> Or bends with the remover to remove:
> O, no! it is an ever-fixed mark.
> That looks on tempests, and is never shaken,
> It is the star to every wandering bark,
> Whose worth's unknown, although his height be taken.[22]

They know who they are. They know of my boundless gratitude for their being who they are, and for the ways, far beyond their realizing, in which they have blessed me.

Above all there are the precious few in the intimate family circle: son Dave, and daughter-in-law, Sue; their children, Kathryn and Jon; daughter, Loey; and Joe, no longer with us, but still a lively presence.

And, dearest of all, Eleonore. Prodigal in her caring for people, to the point of abandon; lavish in gift giving; quick to tears, of grief or of laughter; feisty in conviction; defender of the faith in women's liberation, long before it became a burning issue; troubler of Israelites mired in musty, unexamined tradition; vilifier of hypocrisy; confidante of the weak and wavering; kindler of sparks; gourmet cook and exemplary hostess; game player of game players; thoroughly unreliable when it comes to maps and directions; vacillating in handling trivia, Gibraltar-firm in matters of moment.

The two of us determined to build a home where one could come and go at will. So, it has been a habitation where merriment is a mark of maturity, where protest can be heard, where pain is bravely born and conflict accepted, if never fully resolved; where prejudice is outlawed, and sins are forgiven. That we have fallen short is openly admitted, but what we have accomplished can be credited to Eleonore, far more than she would allow or consider possible. To borrow Alan Paton's phrase, there is a brightness about her, light slanting into the dark places through the cracks and crannies of her lively presence. *Enthusiasm*—it's her most distinguishing mark, and I use the word in the full sense of its derivation: *en theos*, "in God!"

The Sacrament of Solitude

When it comes to describing personality types, I belong, broadly speaking, to the "loner" category. For one thing, I require more time for myself than many people. It's the way I am put together, and I finally accepted the fact that there's nothing wrong with it. I try to watch out for its negative side, though not always successfully, as my friends and family may point out when I rudely withdraw from a conversation and disappear in a fog of preoccupation. I try to guard against such self-indulgence, remembering that there are social conventions to be honored and that, while the hermit in me must be respected, I have obligations to others.

Nonetheless, I covet the times when I can be alone, free from the pressures of "group dynamics," free to be quiet, free to listen for voices that can be heard only in the sacraments of solitude and silence.

In this celebration of solitude, I think of Jacob in the Old Testament. He is one of my favorite Bible characters. He was a brash wheeler and dealer, a shady con man of the first order. Without missing a beat, he talked his brother Esau out of his birthright. Then, with the help of his mother, who was no slouch at the same game, he deceitfully secured his aged father's coveted blessing. But this time all hell broke loose, and in the ensuing uproar, Jacob realized that he had overplayed his hand. His mother packed him off to her brother Laban's place until things cooled off. But he stayed longer than planned. Uncle Laban proved to be an opponent worthy of his own talents in trickery and deceit, and for fourteen years they went at each other. In the end, Jacob won out, walking away with his loot. He became rich and powerful, with many herds and servants, the record tells us.

But one day, his past began to catch up with him. News came that Esau, whom he hadn't seen for years and who also had prospered, was on his way to meet him. Jacob was alarmed and on guard. No telling how an encounter with an aggrieved brother might turn out. The years with all their layers of smooth talk and fast thinking began to fall away. Jacob knew that he was up against one of those watershed moments that we all have to face. He knew that he had to have it out with himself, and with God, before he could meet Esau in the morning. So, we read in the record: "Jacob was left alone. And there was one who wrestled with him until daybreak."

"Jacob was left alone." At long last, he acknowledged

an elemental truth about himself, and about each one of us, for that matter: an ultimate solitariness, a final standing alone. It was then that Jacob's true character emerged, and he took on a new spiritual stature.

I live by fellowship, by communion with others. I know that and celebrate it. I am dependent upon other people, drawing unbelievable strength from my relationships with them. But there comes the time when I can no longer substitute relationships, however precious and supportive, for confronting myself in solitude. As Henri Nouwen has said, we may go to almost any lengths to avoid facing our basic human aloneness. Because for all our reliance upon community and the deep communion it often generates, we are, in the end, alone in this life.

Søren Kierkegaard put it dramatically when he pictured any one of us at the end of our earthly journey. There you will be, he said, standing utterly alone, with all the silence of eternity about you, and a voice will ask you only one question, "How did you manage your relationships with yourself?"

Thoreau put it more whimsically. He said it's like the person who, more and more aware of an emptiness in the inner life, goes more frequently and more desperately to the post office. But you can be quite sure, he said, that the person who walks away with the most letters hasn't heard from himself or herself this long time!"

"Jacob was left alone." And in that aloneness for the first time, he not only came to terms with himself but, more important, laid his conniving, self-centered self open to the influence of a brooding Presence that had never let him out of sight. As my poet friend Arnold Kenseth said once of Jacob: what marks him, wily and corrupted though he is, is that

> he goes in search of himself and his deepest meaning as a human being. But what is even more remarkable emerges when [in order] to discover himself, he casts himself up

against the terrifying mystery of God. Modern men and women, equally possessed by their possessions and corrupted by power, seem to lack Jacob's perception.

The fact is that there are no bypasses around the experience of stubbornly trying to wrestle the truth about ourselves out of One who knows us better than we do ourselves, and who goes on loving us, even when in our lovelessness we have given up on ourselves. More than once I have hesitated to take the next step I knew I had to take toward health and wholeness: a solitary engagement with "the terrifying mystery of God." Midnight wrestling in solitude is painful. Mine has been, like Jacob's. And, like his, I'll always bear the scars of it. We read in the story that during Jacob's struggle his hip was thrown out of joint, and he limped as he went back to take up his life again. But whatever else, he was sure of one thing: he limped into the sunrise!

I have been the beneficiary of solitude in other ways. It gives me the opportunity to appropriate new insights about myself and situations that come only under its conditions. It's the old business of allowing my mind and spirit to lie fallow for a time in order that the wisdom and poise I need have a chance to seep in on their own. They can't be crammed in under pressure or by a dogged exercise of the will.

I heard about a woman who became interested in jade and wanted to learn everything she could about it. She signed up for a course taught by a well-known expert in the field. There were twelve lessons. "How do they go?" she asked. The instructor said, "It's very simple. You come every week for an hour, and by the last session I guarantee that you will know how to evaluate jade." The woman faithfully attended all the sessions. Each week the same thing happened: the instructor gave each member of the class a sample stone and left the room. That was it. As the weeks went on, our friend's irritation mounted, and after the eleventh session, she exploded to a friend: "That instructor is a phony; he's no expert. Look what I get for all the time and money I've spent. Eleven hours, and all I've done is to hold a stupid piece of jade in my hands!" Last session was the same procedure, and she said to her friend, "You see, he has not only wasted my time and money for eleven hours, but in the last hour, to add insult to injury, he gives me a fake piece of jade!"

My most urgent need for solitude is the opportunity it provides for me to work at maintaining the deep, inner core of integrity that defines and affirms *me,* the unique individual I am. Consider this chunk of wisdom by Dag Hammarskjöld chipped from the granite of his experience. "To preserve the silence within, amid all the noise. To remain open and quiet, a moist humus in the fertile darkness where the rain falls and the grain ripens, no matter how many tramp across the parade ground in whirling dust under an arid sky."

Deep down, far below the surface where I spend my busy days in a crossfire of conflicting opinions and shifting values, there is an inviolable place where I know who I am, where I can possess my soul in as much peace as possible, where I try to keep faith with honor and dreams, "a moist humus in the fertile darkness." Solitude is required if I am to cultivate that precious patch of soil.

Like everyone else, I am tempted, of course, to look for an easier way. I know what the alternatives are. One is to scurry to a particular part of the parade ground where, I am told, there are packaged answers. Another is to turn to one of the several forms of authoritarian religion where I can expect a divinely authenticated book or institution to provide simple answers to appallingly difficult questions. Another is simply to "go back" to spiritual formulas and guarantees of an earlier day, to deify some aspect of a dead past.

I neglect seasons of solitude at my peril. For instinctively I know that an elemental kind of aloneness goes with being human, something built into our very existence, something in the marrow of our bones that comes with us when we are born into the world. Again, it takes a poet to put a truth like that in such a way that it cannot be overlooked. Here is Robert Frost working at it.

> Summer was past and day was past.
> Somber clouds in the west were massed.
> Out in the porch's sagging floor
> Leaves got up in a coil and hissed,
> Blindly struck at my knee and missed.
> Something sinister in the tone
> Told me my secret must be known:
> Word I was in the house alone
> Somehow must have gotten abroad,
> Word I was in my life alone,
> Word I had no one left but God.[23]

That may be a dark way, perhaps, of coming at a fundamental truth about my life. But it brings its own light. For it is a secret that God and I share, and no darkness I experience can ever blot that out. An ultimate aloneness simply goes with my being human, but the feelings of loneliness that go with it are never an unbearable desolation. Rather such aloneness is, essentially, the sacrament of solitude, another gift of grace, bringing with it the promise of new life, like the burgeoning of spring out of the dark and cold of winter.

CHAPTER 5

Carrying My Chalice

The poet Yeats once spoke about the crucial importance for him of bearing safely the precious chalice of his own being.

I choose Yeats's words as a metaphor for rounding off these reflections on my liberation journey. It is a telling way of assessing how responsibly I have carried my chalice, this unique and precious vessel of being that was put into my keeping. It *is* unique; I have come to accept and celebrate that. However fragile and faulted, whatever its shape or sheen, it is what I have been able to make of the raw material put into my keeping to mold into a vessel of purpose and meaning. It is, as well, the only means I have had for transmitting a Word that is not one of my words and a Truth that towers above my collections of expedient and clever truths.

I have carried my chalice over many kinds of terrain, through all sorts of weather. There have been swamplands and miles of tangled underbrush. There have been stretches of desert that I thought would never end. There has been exposure to scouring winds on high, rocky ridges; and there have been gentle grassy slopes, cool woods, sunlit meadows, and restful nights under the silent stars. Frequently, I have stumbled and spilled some of the precious contents, or I have dropped it and scratched its finish. Several times I have mislaid it among the clutter of busyness. I have been known to carry it in the wrong direction!

What is certain is that I still have it in my keeping, and this, itself, is an infallible sign of grace.

For the most part, I find that success or failure as a chalice bearer has depended upon my capacity to handle the element of tension. Tension is an essential ingredient in a person's intent and effort to stay alive as long as one lives. As a member of a community of retired religious workers, I have ample opportunity to observe the variety of ways there are of handling tension. There are those "seniors" who, after a career of heavy commitment and involvement in the people and issues that crowd the human scene, say that they are entitled to a tension-free existence. They have earned it, they will tell you, and apparently they are content with a daily round of pleasurable, nonstressful, "retirement"-type activities. (If that is their honest choice, so be it, although I am a little uneasy about what any of us can claim to have "earned." Nor do I quite understand why retirement and longevity, in themselves, are valid claims for exemption from tension.

One thing I *am* sure of is that among the most "alive," most fulfilled, happiest people I know are those in their seventies, eighties, and nineties who still kindle fires and set off rockets of passionate conviction. More often than not, they create tension and send waves of discontent billowing through the beloved community. In sharp contrast, there are those for whom the now classic comment made by Dorothy Parker is applicable. Upon being informed that a prominent public figure had died, she said, "How can they tell?"

Tension Between Am and Ought to Be

For one thing, there has always been for me the tension between who I am and what I ought to be. For years on end, I was motivated by an overriding sense of *oughtness*. A muscular, domineering Puritan of unlovely mien rode my back. How he, or she, got there had much to do with the Calvinistic strain in my upbringing. Oughtness, to be sure, is fundamental to all moral behavior. Society is kept on balance because there are enough morally responsible people around doing precisely what they *ought* to do. But in my case, oughtness got out of hand, assumed unhealthy control. For example, I took it for granted that something I very much *wanted* to do, only for the reason of *wanting* to do it, was invalid if not downright sinful. Certainly it smacked of blatant self-indulgence, and all such behavior was outlawed by fidelity to higher, more noble claims. I was never free to be *all* of myself. There were areas of experience that never were explored. There were pastures where I never dared to wander. There was no "tonic of wildness."

One thing can be said, of course, for the prevailing Puritan climate in which I grew up. Whatever else it does, it keeps you mindful of your limitations, never allowing you to think of yourself more highly than you ought to think. God knows how mindful I was of my limitations! I was unhealthily modest, convinced, as Winston Churchill said once of Clement Atlee, that, indeed, I had a lot to be modest about! I see things differently now. The kind of stuffy oughtness I lived by, together with a propensity to accommodate too readily to other people's ideas and convictions, kept me from becoming a whole, authentic person. I can identify with Frederic ("the slave of duty") in Gilbert and Sullivan's *The Pirates of Penzance*, who, liberated from the bondage of his apprenticeship, tests out his new-found freedom on Major General Stanley's bevy of beautiful daughters:

> "Oh, is there not one maiden breast
> Which does not feel the moral beauty
> Of making wordly interest
> Subordinate to sense of duty?"

I'm better at honoring priorities than I used to be: listening to an opera, browsing in a bookstore, working at stained glass, as against attending a meeting with low-level interest or tidying up my files. Some of my friends think I have a long way to go. They may be right, but I'm not sure they understand how far I have come!

Tension Between the Person and the Professional

There has been the tension between who I am, essentially, as a person and as a "professional" in my career, that is, when I am performing the functions of a trained preacher, pastor, teacher, and administrator. Obviously, certain distinctions between essence and function are expected. Church members quite rightly require their minister to adhere to professional standards: acute sensitivity to people's feelings and situations, confidentiality, ruthless honesty, tactfulness, better-than-average handling of the English language, and, above all, overriding compassion.

There are occasions, however, where "professional" behavior simply takes over, and people lose sight of the bona fide human being hidden behind the ministerial front. Paul Tournier alerted me to being aware of this danger by distinguishing between the "person" and the "personage." The latter incorporates a set of mannerisms and a cultivated style of presence deemed appropriate for professional certification. Consider the minister who in everyday conversation holds up his or her end of it with perfectly normal intonation and inflection but once in the pulpit, preaching or praying, takes on a honeyed "holy" tone, presumably considered desirable when speaking of holy things. The voice rumbles, soars, and quivers as though such were required to gain a hearing in the courts of the Almighty.

Or there is the minister who oozes charisma at every clerical pore. I may be overly sensitive on the subject, and I have nothing against ministers who have a thoroughly genuine personal magnetism about them. Bless their hearts and the natural radiance that so winsomely draws people into their circle of caring! At its best, charisma is a channel of grace, life touching life with disarming purity. But at its worst, it is a form of shameless exploitation, sometimes establishing a personality cult. In instances I have known, so much attention was focused on the minister that for years after his departure people still referred to a particular congregation as "Dr. So-and-So's church." That it never *was* Dr. So-and-So's church seems to have escaped everyone's attention, including Dr. So-and-So!

More than once, I allowed the "professional" to obscure the person that is supposed to be me. There are the times I tried to keep my own vulnerability a secret, not wanting to admit to people that I hurt in the same places they hurt, grow angry the way they do, need the same satisfactions they need, am weak when I should be strong, cowardly when I should be courageous. They suspected all those things about me, I am sure; but the fact that for supposed professional reasons I could not, or would not, openly admit them was a barrier between us.

I think of the times, in the earlier years especially, when I was successful in cloistering my interior life, keeping it what I considered a necessary and safe distance from my functioning as a professional. Whatever might be going on in my head or heart I considered to be exclusively *my* business, and my exposure of it would result in diminished effectiveness as a pastor, an exemplar of the faith, a "father figure," or however else members of the flock thought of me. In the eyes of some, I was thought to be above the battle, by birth or training possessing a larger store of patience and poise than lay people, equipped with an abnormally high boiling point and with an awesome capacity for walking a second, even a third mile. It was taken for granted that these and other uniquely Christian virtues come with the territory and somehow were officially validated in the act of ordination.

Needless to say, I haven't shucked all such nonsense, but after much trial and error, I have been able to sort things out. In any event, looking back over the years, I am more persuaded than ever that authenticity for a minister lies in ultimate reliance on the person at the core.

The folk singer Mason Williams once told about making

a new recording of one of his songs because he could sing it better, the reason being that he had been working on himself rather than on his singing. In the end, he said, you have to go to work on where the music comes from.

The "person" and the "personage": keeping the two separated is a slippery business. On the one hand, there is the trained professional: pulpit-trained, voice-trained, pastor-trained, organization-trained, trained-trained! Evelyn Underhill's commentary on Hans Christian Andersen's tale of the emperor with no clothes is to the point. Far more dismaying than his radical breach of propriety, she said, is the sight of a magnificent display of clothes and no emperor!

On the other hand there is the *me* at the core of my being—the irreducible, elemental me—lumps, liabilities, and everything else, the only trustworthy bearer of my chalice.

Tension Between Pastoral and Prophetic Roles

Again, I have had to deal with the tension between being a pastor, as well as a responsible member of the economic and social system of which I am a part, and my commitment to the prophetic role of a minister in a world marked by injustice.

During a retreat for ministers that I was leading, we got around to discussing the mandate of maintaining an Old Testament prophetic stance in ministry. There was general agreement that such a stance had to be taken, but there was hesitation on the part of several members of the group as to the matter of timing. One young minister, newly arrived in a church, said that he knew that eventually he'd have to address a serious issue of social justice in the community, but he felt that he should wait until he knew the members better, until, as he put it, he had had time to prepare the ground. He'd be a good pastor first, he said, then a prophet.

Bless his heart! I know what he was talking about. It is far, however, from being the last word on the subject. But you can't necessarily condone it, either. Loving pastoral care and a prophetic witness are two deeply rooted marks of authentic ministry. And the tension between them is a third! Clearly, there are times in the life of a church when tension must be loosened and breathing space provided. But there are other times when tension must deliberately be tightened, when an issue must be addressed head-on, and when the appropriateness of time and place has little or nothing to do with it. The words of Micah may not indicate the lectionary for the coming Sunday, but the coming Sunday may be precisely the time to deal with them: "The Lord has a controversy with the people; the Lord will contend with Israel." The subject is likely to offend a number of the saints, but bypassing it might involve a violation of ordination vows.

At a time in this nation when business, political institutions, individuals, and even churches seem more concerned about improving their image than turning their imagination loose for the shaping of a more just society and a world of peace, the prophetic imperative is all the more crucial. When the shaping of public opinion dances to the tunes of Madison Avenue, and an administration bases its foreign policy on paranoia regarding the Soviet Union and periodically injects stiff doses of 101 percent patriotism into the national bloodstream, the prophetic voice needs to be heard more clearly than ever.

My own strong feelings on the subject were confirmed by what happened to me and my ministry in a New England congregation. It was a collision between minister and people over the issue of racial justice. To be sure, there was general agreement in the congregation that preaching on such a theme was appropriate, though uncomfortable. In fact, I was urged to do so by an articulate minority in the membership. But preaching sermons is relatively safe. It was my becoming more deeply involved and the confrontational style I adopted at one point that precipitated the crisis. I invited a militant black leader to interpret for us the stringent demands of the "Black Manifesto," which became an important focusing point for the civil rights issue in the late sixties. That occasion, and subsequent discussions, proved to be far more than the majority of the congregation was prepared to handle. The people, of course, were not unique. They were members of a church that, like many others, had, for years, studiously avoided the invasion of any upsetting, controversial issues into its well-insulated existence.

It was a time of severe pain for all of us, minister and people, made more so by the publicity that resulted: the front page in the *Boston Globe* and discussion in a denominational journal. It is still painful to talk about. Not all my handling of the situation was exemplary. I readily admit that. Some individuals were needlessly wounded. There were options for alternative action that I chose not to take. For all of that, I was convinced that it was one of those times when truth had to be turned into an event. In the life of that particular church, at that moment in history, under those singular circumstances, I believed there was only one thing for me to do: resign my ministry. I did so, and the rest of the professional staff resigned with me. Privately, I hoped they wouldn't, but they had consciences to deal with, too. Along with their support came that of a number of church members, family members, and close friends.

I have sometimes wondered why I didn't hear from more of my colleagues in ministry. A few expressed their concern for me in touching ways, and I shall always treasure their drawing close. Several younger ministers, under similar pressure, expressed their gratitude for what I had done and said that, in some measure, I spoke for them. But, by and large, there was little reaction that personally touched me. I suspect that many ministers simply disapproved of what I had done but refrained, for one reason or another, from letting me know. Others, probably, saw it as an uncomfortable, awkward state of affairs they couldn't handle or didn't wish to handle. I'm sure that my wondering about it was because of my elemental need to have some people simply stand beside me, whether they agreed with me or not. It was a lonely, lonely time, and I waited for notes and telephone calls that didn't come.

My friend Joseph Williamson talks about the prophetic imperative in a telling way. For Christians, he says, it's a matter of locale, of knowing the place where they are to take their stand. And that, he says, is usually on the edges of the human situation, out on one of its boundaries where suffering is most acute, where the issues of justice are most urgent, where peace is most endangered. It is there, on some exposed frontier, that God waits for us to join a new exodus, a long-postponed liberation march out of bondage into freedom. To be sure, God also waits for us in the quietness and seclusion of our sanctuaries—to be still, to renew our spirits, to hear a healing, saving word according to our individual needs. Helping its members cultivate a deep, sustaining personal faith is priority business for an authentic church, just so long as the end result is not a vaporous spirituality that promises insulation against the troublesome, controversial issues of society. As a matter of fact, the biblical brand of spirituality implies just the opposite. It pushes us to a God-haunted frontier where our commission is abundantly plain: "to preach the Good News to the poor . . . to proclaim liberty to the captives and recovery of sight to the blind, to set free the oppressed."

Such frontiers are usually uncomfortably close by. They may be the local supermarket, one's place of business, the children's school, even the Sunday morning congregation. It may be the frontier I have become more and more aware of these recent years, where courageous women keep tightening the tension between the exercise of their unconditioned, God-granted freedom and the crippling bondage of dinosaur-age patriarchy. They ask the rest of us to understand their journey and to share it with them wherever and whenever we can. If we do so, we shall come to recognize the depth and sweep of what women are talking about when they speak of their liberation. To take it seriously, says Rosemary Ruether, is to work for a fundamental reconstruction of a hierarchical pattern in human society in which males are accorded a superior, and women an inferior, role. We have to listen to women's anger about that and take it in utter seriousness. When they remind us of Jesus' words that in God there is neither male nor female, we have no choice but to believe him and simply accept that inherently radical concept of human relations. For women are not simply petitioning us to clean up our language or make some adjustments that will give them more breathing space. They want none of these things if, once attained, they are still part of a society, or of a church, that is under the sovereignty of patriarchy, where they are regarded and treated as second-class citizens. Nor are they prepared to accept offers of assistance that smack of paternalism. Actually, what they are demanding is that men get out of their way, for they understand, just as black people understand, that they, themselves, must do most of the back-breaking work of their liberation.

There is another, even more hazardous, frontier. It is where we have the obligation to stand beside our lesbian sisters and gay brothers who have with honesty and courage acknowledged their homosexual orientation. They desperately need the affirmation and support of all of us who refuse to think of them as sinners in need of forgiveness or as basically unhealthy people who can be set straight by professional therapy. There is no subject in our society or in the life of our churches that we approach with more ignorance, fear, and hostility. How many of us there are who still come to it with inexcusable ignorance or sickening prejudice! However tight the tension may become in dealing with it, we cannot any longer put off getting our heads straight, our hearts opened, and our theology corrected. Up until now, God has been patient with our blindness and intransigence. How much longer we can count on it is an open question!

Tension Between Productivity and Creativity

Finally, I have tried to keep alive a necessary tension between productivity and creativity. Looking back over the years of ministry, it struck me one day how much of the time I had spent being a *producer* for the most part—of sermons, services of worship, courses of study, agenda for meetings, weekly columns, and all the rest.

To be sure, there is a production-line aspect to ministry. To a degree, ministers live by clock and calendar. The Word must be proclaimed regularly and in good order. If meetings are to be productive, they must be carefully planned in advance, convened and adjourned in good time, and accurately reported. The same goes for effective pastoral work and innumerable appointments to be met. I have known ministers, of course, who apparently considered themselves liberated from all such regimentation, as they saw it. They strolled through a typical busy week. It was refreshing to observe their relaxed style and their refusal to be bulldozed by a schedule. Some of them did well enough, largely, I suspect, because of personal charm and a certain charisma. But for others, their off-hand, catch-as-catch can approach wound up in ineffectiveness and mediocrity. Spontaneity and élan with little relation to goals can be wearing, singularly unproductive, and, in the end, rather tiresome.

Since having to produce is inevitable, my overriding concern is to manage it with all the flair, the fire, and lilt of genuine creativity I can summon. One way is to shift the focus of whatever is at hand from task to people. Take, for example, the reporting of the thousand and one meetings to be attended—"minutes," to be exact. My unabridged Webster says: "Minutes: an official record of what was said and done at a meeting." Plain enough. But the definition is subject to variables: capacities (or limitations) for accurate reporting; the degree of complexity of matters under discussion; the disposition, temperament, and even the literary aspirations of the secretaries who write and respectfully submit their reports. I once knew the secretary of an organization who poured into her minutes the residue of her frustrated dreams to write a best seller. With an exquisite sense of detail, she laced her chronicling of the business at hand with titillating descriptions and spicy observations. Her minutes were often the only bright spot on the agenda! They were eagerly anticipated and occasionally received with a round of applause! The only trouble with them was that they conveyed relatively little sense of what had transpired at the meeting!

I accept the need for the traditional type of minutes—who was present, who wasn't, votes that were taken, and so on. As long as we have to have them, however, let them be concise and crisp. My deeper concern is for a different kind of record keeping. As a matter of fact, I'm convinced that in order to have a reliable account of what takes place at a meeting, we need *two* sets of minutes. One is the conventional record of personnel and actions set down in one-two-three, no-nonsense style. But another set is required; the first cannot be a complete or even accurate "record of what was said and done." Because, sometimes, what was said was precisely left unsaid in words. Why, for example, was Mr. A silent at a particular juncture? Why did Miss B leave the room at that moment? (It may not have been the generally assumed reason.) Why did Mrs. C obviously avoid answering a certain question? Did Mr. D come close to losing his temper? Why that uneasy shifting of chairs, those dark looks, that muttering? Or what about the two people who didn't say a word all evening?

Far more is involved, of course, than this or that set of minutes. It is the old, often overlooked aspect of all human enterprises: not simply *what* happens when people are in communication with each other, but also, and perhaps more importantly, *how* something happens. And quite frequently, how something happens is precisely *what* happens! The kind of second set of minutes I speak of is not likely to be published. It doesn't have to be if, as the apostle Paul put it, it is written "not on tablets of stone [or pink mimeograph paper], but on tablets of human hearts."

Some years ago in New England, I had a friend who was a painter of distinction. Her work was essentially traditional—landscapes, weather-beaten barns, still life. One day, when she was well into her eighties, she took a critical look at a stack of canvasses in her studio and had, she said, a sense of weariness. In a sense, she was saying that much of what she had been doing was to "produce" paintings that people would admire and hopefully buy, that some of her native creativity had eroded. She did an abrupt turnabout: she decided to experiment with various forms of impressionism. It took her a while, she said, to get the hang of it, but even her early efforts in the new style have a freshness and vitality about them. The tension she felt between the traditional and the "far out," as some critics called it, renewed the springs of creativity. I think of that renewal when I glance at *High-Over Farm* on our living room wall.

In all of this, of course, there is the wisdom of what has already been spoken of—ground left fallow. So much of the time we insist that every square foot of space, energy, and time be carefully planned in advance, put on schedule, monitored, computerized, if possible, and reported on regularly, nothing wasted, nothing left to chance. In doing so, we are likely to bypass a crucial ingredient in all creativity— the capacity of life to renew itself, in its own time, in its own way, like the good earth, unplanted for a season, left to the beneficient mercies of sun and rain, wind and frost, and the silent sweep of cloud shadow across the empty furrows.

So it is with these lives we feel compelled, sometimes driven to be in charge of at every turn. It has taken me years to get hold of that truth, to know that there are times when I need to be off the scene, to put management into other hands for a season. The impulses of creation, itself, must be given the chance to have their inscrutable way with me. There are rainfall, sunlight, and winds of the Spirit that, praise God! are beyond my supervision.

It is, as a matter of fact, ultimate wisdom required for chalice bearing. I have accented the business of deliberately tightening tension when circumstances demand it. As long as I am on the scene, I expect that pressure to be laid against me. Nonetheless, in these later years, I have come to appreciate, as well, the importance of releasing tension. To be able to manage that release is one of the distinctive marks of maturity. It needn't mean the surrender of life-deep convictions or the end of sturdy, even feisty, witnessing to the truth now and then. But it does mean an ultimate sitting loose on unresolved issues, in society or in my own life, on whatever lies ahead for me in the shadowy shapes of an unknown tomorrow. To say it another way, it is a matter of acceptance, even accepting things I may have considered unacceptable. At any rate, here in the autumn years I publish my list of "acceptables."

Accepting the Past

I shall try to accept the past gracefully. As many of us can testify, the past forgets its place now and then. I honor it, and I have to transfer from yesterday's account all the assets it has that will enrich the present and the future. There is all that I have learned from defeats and hard times in general. There are the priceless testimonies of older, wiser folk who have been on the same journey. There is the heady wisdom to be acquired from younger people who are not tightly bound to moss-covered tradition. There are the memories of sturdy lives that have touched and blessed mine. And there are the actions and ministries of my own about which I have good feelings and which I can justifiably celebrate.

But then there are the liabilities. There are the ghastly mistakes in judgment I made about people and situations. There are all the things I left undone when only a little effort on my part would have seen them accomplished. There are the requests to which I said yes when I should have said no. There are the risks I didn't take when risk taking was precisely what was called for. There are the times when without good reason, I put expectations of my job before those of my family. There are the situations that needed my attention and that I should have waded into without hesitation but, because I knew it would have troubled the waters, I dodged. There are the cries for help that I heard clearly enough but that I ignored on claims of busyness. There are all the good intentions that never developed hands and feet. There is much more. So I sift through the past, salvaging what is worth keeping and trying to deal with the remainder in a no-nonsense way. Eventually I have to stand the past up in front of me and say: "Look, you've had your day. By and large, it was a good day, and I am grateful for all that was part of it which has benefited me. But your sun has set now, and I have to say to you regarding your claims, 'That was yesterday.' I accept the ways you have influenced me, but only up to a point. Beyond that, anything you have to say is meddling."

I understand now enough of what went on in by-gone years to put it into perspective. The sands of compassion have drifted over it all, ribs and spars of shipwreck buried along the outer coast of my days. Now and then, a neap tide and stormy surf will expose bits and pieces of it, but not for long, for the sea quickly reclaims its own. Moreover, most of what I have room for now is what I have stored against the graying years. There are fragments of gold I have come upon, flaking into dust but still glowing dully in the remembering of shadowed, worrisome experiences. There are a few finely cut jewels that still flash fire and require the best setting I can afford to honor them. There are rough chunks of color that will never be shaped or polished, that exist just as they are for my personal delight, which is reason enough for cherishing them. There are dark, disfigured forms to remind me of the wisdom that accrues only through suffering. There are snatches of music—the brassy blare of trumpet tunes, the heartbeat of a spiritual, the lilt of a Viennese waltz. There are words that invoke a beauty and a blessing beyond my comprehension, those of Shakespeare's sonnets, for example. There are images indelibly etched on the screen of memory: a nor'easter slashing the dunes on the Great Beach of Cape Cod, or a blaze of October maples consuming a New Hampshire hillside.

Accepting Limitations

I shall try to accept gracefully whatever limitations lengthened years or unavoidable circumstances impose upon me. For example, there is my steady loss of hearing. I tried to ignore it at first, saw it as a minor irritant that I could accommodate to easily. But the loss steadily increased, and I finally accepted a major task of accommodation. One price of it is the grieving that goes with any serious loss. Working through that, I discovered, is as important as securing the best hearing aids available. My audiologist agrees, but he also urged me to keep a sense of humor about it, even though the matter is not funny. I agree. There is a certain comic relief when what is presumably a sensible observation, made in all sobriety, filters through my hearing apparatus as sheer nonsense, with my response having no relevance whatever to the conversation in progress!

Equally important, it is necessary for me to accept, to come to terms with, certain limitations that are ingrained, that are part of the essential me. I have inherited some of them; others have developed because of carelessness or negligence on my part. Whatever their origin, these obvious limitations are simply evidence of inborn perverseness, of what Paul calls the "sin which dwells within me [Romans 7:20]." There are those who bridle at such language, considering it quite unhealthy. ("Haven't we got beyond all that 'sin' stuff? I'm tired of being referred to as a 'sinner'," and so on and on). For me, it's simply being brutally realistic to acknowledge it, knowing myself as well as I do.

Take, for example, some of my unlovely social traits that are often a trial and embarrassment to those who love me and, I suppose, to those who don't love me, as well.

One is my downright snobbishness when it comes to my tastes in matters aesthetic. It's not that the matter of taste has a moral dimension to it. I cannot feel guilty about what I like or don't like. It is, rather, that in expressing my opinion about a piece of music or a book, I sometimes convey an impression that my judgment is particularly pure and of a higher order than that of those who differ with me. It's like people who, quite unlike me, are the "bird-song-at-dawn" type, who rise each day between five and six o'clock to take a walk. They have every right to such practices. All I object to is their subtle intimation that, after all, early rising is just slightly more virtuous than lying abed until seven-thirty or eight!

Or, consider what is sometimes taken as my disdain for playing games. This is an especially sensitive subject in our family, for whom every vacation becomes a kind of casino—each member, deck of cards in hand, roaming about, on a constant hunt for a round of this or that! I am clearly in the minority. I don't take to games readily. For one thing, my competitive instinct is minus zero. Also, my reaction time is snail-paced. Roll six dice in one of the family's favorite games, and I need pad and pencil to calculate the throw. The difficulty people have with me is not my disdain; it is my ineptitude and lack of flair for the sporting instinct. To escape being a social outcast and to fulfill certain social obligations (though I have difficulty in seeing game playing as an obligation!), I have become accomplished at pretending to enjoy the games we play, and since this seems to satisfy my fellow players, I leave it at that.

What all this adds up to is the necessity to accept my particular assortment of limitations and, except for observing the restraints of civility and kindness, conclude that, for the most part, any basic changes are not likely to take place. Now and then I hear the voice of the old Puritan I used to live with telling me that I "ought" to work harder on ridding myself of my limitations, but his voice grows fainter and fainter as the years pass. Whatever "oughtness" is left has to do with putting liabilities and things that can't be changed in their place and getting on with the more important business of celebrating, even exploiting, my assets, which I've come to accept as sizable!

Put it down to a lack of ambition, perhaps. But for me, as the years lengthen, ambition takes on a new coloration. I have questions, for example, about some of my fellow "seniors." It's ambition, they say, that keeps them alive and running. First place or, at best second, is still within their reach. Maybe so. But I have made note of a salty chip of wisdom that showed up in an interview with the opera singer Lucia Popp, now past the peak of her career but still an artist of distinction. She was talking about maintaining a high level of excellence throughout one's career. But, she said, eventually you have to learn to say no. "A young singer," she said, "starts out very ambitious. OK, so you get ahead. But along the way, you begin to set other priorities for your life. A person who stays very ambitious to the end is, I think, not fully mature."

Accepting Unanswered Questions

I shall try to accept gracefully an accumulation of unanswered questions. There is a fierce hunger in the world for answers, particularly in a time as threatening and precarious as ours. People look everywhere for them. Preachers, says Frederick Buechner, are under a special pressure. The *answer* is what people have come to church to hear. The preacher has to give an answer because everybody else is giving answers.

> Transcendental meditation is an answer, and the Democratic party is an answer, or the Republican party, and acupuncture and acupressure are answers, and so are natural foods, yogurt, and brown rice. Yoga is an answer

and transactional analysis and jogging. The pressure on the preacher is to promote the Gospel, to sell Christ as an answer that outshines all the other answers.[1]

The trouble with all of this is, of course, that there are no valid answers that can point to a resolution of a situation until we know the right questions to ask about it. And the right questions are sometimes more than we are up to. As Buechner, again, has put it, "The sheltering word can be spoken only after the word that leaves us without a roof over our heads." And that is precisely the word vast numbers of people need to hear, including, I suspect, some of us with our own self-certified "answers." I can see us all, standing there, in the pitiless glare of the truth, stripped of all cozy, comforting clichés, shifting uneasily from one foot to the other, looking for a hiding place, as the biting questions come, one after another. What do you who are well fed, well housed, living bountifully on an assured income know about poor people, anyway? Do you still cling to the notion that most of them are shiftless, lazy, lacking in ambition, and, by choice, dependent on government welfare programs?

Do you have any idea at all what life is like for those men and women who have publicly and courageously acknowledged their homosexual orientation and because of that are excluded from job opportunities and all kinds of meaningful relationships? Have you any notion of what it is like to be looked upon as "unclean," as a potential child molester, or simply as a sinner in need of repentance and forgiveness by your fellow Christians?

Do you know what it is like to be a woman committed to the Christian ministry and with top qualifications for it, whose application is set aside only because of a persistent, suffocating system of patriarchy? Do you know what it is to be a black family whose children are deprived of the same quality of education available to white youngsters in a nearby suburban community?

It may be that after a ruthless exposure to deep, underlying questions and a thorough exposure of our ignorance and prejudices, we shall be able to hear and to understand the "sheltering word." Even then, hearing it, understanding it, working tirelessly to implement it in disciplined programs of action, there will come the time when we are no longer on the scene. Yet there is still so much unaccomplished, so many goals not met, so many of our fellow humans still in bondage. Then is the time of acceptance, of quiet commitment of all we have stood and worked for into the loving hands of God.

It is my faith that, even though our efforts on behalf of justice and peace seem to have so small effect, God hears the poignant cry of the consecrated that rises night and day, age after age, from this broken bleeding earth, this God who moves steadily toward the answers that must be given in the fullness of time.

It's there in the closing scene of George Bernard Shaw's magnificent play *Saint Joan*—all the pity and the hope of it. The last rays of light gather in a blinding radiance and fall on Joan's upraised face, as she prays: "O God, that madest this beautiful earth, when will it be ready to receive thy saints? How long, O Lord, how long?"

Accepting the Flight of Time

Finally, I shall try to accept gracefully the inexorable flight of time. Here in my late seventies, I have a keener awareness of it than ever, and while I have no stressful anxiety about it, I know that there are conditions that I must come to terms with.

The first is to understand and to own the Bible's concept of time as the clue to the way I handle the years remaining. It is in sharp contrast to the fretful, frantic mood of our age. It is caught eloquently in the somber beauty of the ninetieth psalm. Here a poet ponders the passage of time, not with the raucous salute of a New Year's Eve party, but in quiet reflection on our brief, transitory pilgrimage in the light of God's eternity. A mellow sherry, let's say, instead of bubbly champagne! "From everlasting to everlasting thou art god. . . . For a thousand years in thy sight are but as yesterday. . . . So teach us to number our days that we may get a heart of wisdom. [Psalm 90: 2, 4, 12]." Another psalmist adds a postscript, "O God, my times are in thy hand! [Psalm 31: 15]."

Dip into the Bible almost everywhere and you'll find this towering conviction that people's lives are never for a moment out of sight of an all-wise, all-benevolent purpose. It is the confidence Christians have that all of history, even that of our disjointed time, is not a mindlessly unraveling skein of events but a continuum of human experience under the constant scrutiny of a God who will not be deterred from working out an eternal purpose.

There is a parable about the way biblical faith deals with the passing of time in an old clock I once saw in the cathedral in Lund, Sweden. Every day at noon a crowd gathers to watch its "performance." As the minute hand jerks to the dot of twelve, chimes ring, and two tiny pages step out of doors at either side of the face, lift their silver trumpets, and play a lively march tune. Then a procession begins—knights and ladies and three kings. As they pass in front of a niche just below the face of the clock where Mary and Joseph are with the Christ Child, they bow reverently and then disappear through the far doorway.

Whatever biblical faith provides, it is the long view. God has all kinds of time, is not overly concerned with any deadlines I may set. There are broken threads in relationships I'd like to tie together but may not be able to. There are the "dreams deferred," the anxiety about things I'd like to round out before I leave the scene.

The long view doesn't always come easily for older people. But I, for one, am grateful for a measure of composure that comes from accepting the fact that from here on out, my range of choices will be narrowing all the time. The causes I have worked for will not be forgotten or lost because younger, stronger, and probably wiser hands than mine will be working at them, in a different style, at another tempo. Nor do I have to assume that my effectiveness will be all that diminished. In fact, there may be a heightening of my powers as I learn to live more in depth and less on the surface. And without the long view, I am likely to become merely a bundle of aging, frustrated nerves. I know that nonconforming, rebellious young people can be hard to live with at times, but fussy old men and women, peevishly complaining about this or that, are a burden and a dreadful bore!

Certainly, as I live with a sharper sense of time's swift flight, my encounters with the truth become more urgent. I mean, for example, being able to express the truth more forthrightly, to stand by it more openly, to try to embody it more courageously than I ever have before. It is one of the commitments of old age—to say things straight out without hedging or pussyfooting, to be the advocates of those who are having a hard time getting a hearing, or to speak on a minority position that is being ignored or bad-mouthed.

Most important, I can view the prospect of my death with poise and serenity. As a pastor, I sat beside the dying and presided at funerals, memorial services, and burials.

I tried, as best I could, to comfort the bereaved. But I had never really looked death straight in the face until, in the early hours on a cold March morning, suddenly, it was there in the face of our seventeen-year-old son. I watched him closely as the end came, wondering, as I'm sure *he* was, what was happening to him, as he reached out to us for the help we couldn't give. Then it was over—that fast!

In the days following, I skirted a yawning pit of nothingness. I could not summon Dylan Thomas's fierce anger that poured out of him at his father's death:

> Do not go gentle into that good night . . .
> Rage, rage against the dying of the light![2]

In a way, I wish now that I had done just that. It would have been far healthier than what all my native instincts, like fire engines answering an alarm, herded me into doing.

Characteristically, I began to wall in the experience, to beef up my powers of self-control so that my grief would not become public, to contain it within the boundaries of my own private terrain and my professional responsibility: "Trespassers, keep out!" All this in spite of engulfing waves of compassion and comfort that washed over us as a family. Church members and friends, near and distant, kept watch over us for months. Meantime, I retreated more and more into the busyness of a demanding parish ministry.

I have long since given up morbid feelings of guilt about that, but I still have bad feeling about my handling of that bleak stretch of my journey, for I did not keep the faith. I did not keep faith with what I had committed my life to and about which I often preached effectively. I did not keep faith with my family; I withdrew from them at a time when they needed me most. And, what hurts the most, I did not keep faith with my son, who, despite a serious vision handicap, lived with a brightness and buoyancy that put us all to shame.

But there came the day when that particular gray patch turned to white, and belatedly I came to terms with Joe's death and was able to do some honest grieving. We were at a session of our "Shalom" support group. In the course of our life sharing, the subject came up. Eleonore, who, on the whole, had handled the whole business more honestly than I, began to speak out of the depths of her unspeakable pain. With the sensitive coaching and encouragement of our group leader, who suggested that we had never really said good-bye to Joe, engulfed in a flood of tears and sobbing, she proceeded to do just that. The experience shook us all, and when it was over, I realized that I, too, had finally said farewell to my son. Out of it came a poem.

>   Death, again.
>   Now screamed out
>   In all the pain and anger
>   Locked so long

In the tidy cabinets of the heart,
Each marked: "Top secret;
To be opened
On state and stated occasions;
Permission required."

Death, again.
The sneering, sallow face
Pressed against the pane,
Streaked with tears
Of dammed-up grief
And rage; knocking,
Rattling the locks.
Let him in,
But only for his own death-blow
To death.

Death, again.
But never again the same.
No hiding place,
No slinking off, No wound-sucking solace.
For, back of sobs:
A muted trumpet,
A peal of bells, a shout,
A sudden rush of joy—
"No dominion!"

The secret's out!

It is the assurance not only that death has no final word to speak over my life; it is my understanding that all my times are God's time, every day and decade. For me, it means knowing that this lumpy collection of cells, feelings, desires, and spiritual aspirations has an eternal dimension to it. As my friend Roger Hazelton once said, it is to know that I am not being drawn relentlessly toward an endless night by the ticking of a clock, but toward a new and richer fulfillment of life's potential. It is to know that, to a degree, I can master time, that I do not have to nurse yesterday's regret or to pry tomorrow's secret.

In short, I am hedged about, bound and liberated, monitored and motivated by a realm of being transcending my small store of wisdom, gifts, and graces. It goes its own indomitable way—with me when I fall in line with it; without me if I cannot, or will not, heed its summons; and even against me, if in my pride and perversity I set myself against it. And when I come to the outer edge, and darkness begins to close in, it will insist on pronouncing a benediction.

I remember vividly the story of the last recital of one of the great singers of our time, Lotte Lehmann. She had announced that it would be her last public appearance, and unlike many other artist, she meant it! She sang her way gloriously through the planned program, generously added a number of encores, then stepped to the edge of the stage to say that she would sing one more song and that it would be the last. She began Franz Schubert's "Ode to Music." Her voice held until three or four bars before the end, and then it broke. Hand to her eyes, she stood with bowed head while the piano, as the voice of music itself in all its power and purity, brought the song, and the career of a great artist, to an eloquent close.

So here in the afternoon, with dusk not far off, with the strange mix of gaiety and sobriety that is the public secret of Christians, I ponder what my faith has to say about the flight of my remaining days, out of yesterday into the shadowy shapes of tomorrow. Glancing more frequently than usual at the clock by which all my time is set, I make humble and grateful acknowledgment of that which is the center and the final meaning of all history, of all time, of all our lives: the love and the grace of God, which overshadows us, enfolds and supports our lives, from age to age, from birth to death, from daybreak to nightfall!

enormous capacity for listening, and his generous sharing of the treasure of his own personal experience. Most of all, he let me know that he really cared about me, and that my ministry there in Scrub Oak Corners was a fairly important component of Christ's Church.

I cannot be another Fred Fagley; there was only one of him. But I can be Oliver Powell, with all attendant liabilities. I can be with you to talk about you and where you are in your ministry, where it hurts, where it feels good, where it is dark, where it tempts, where it sings. I'm not likely to spill over with wise sayings or sage advice. As one of my colleagues puts it, "I have vacated the role of 'answer man.' I feel comfortable about having limited intelligence." But I do have two ears, and, believe it or not, I do have time.

> There is no substitute for personal presence.
> —Henry Sloane Coffin

On a Sunday morning, years ago, George Buttrick was in the pulpit of New York's Madison Avenue Presybterian Church. Part way through the sermon, he became aware of a disturbance toward the back of the sanctuary. An emotionally distraught woman was sobbing hysterically. He paused briefly, noticing that an usher was hurrying to where the woman was sitting. He resumed the sermon, but the woman refused to leave her place. Suddenly she stood up, and cried out to Dr. Buttrick across the rows of anxious worshipers, "I won't go unless you go with me!" He came down from the pulpit and went straight to her. He put his arm about her, tenderly led her to the narthex, and stayed with her until he put her in the hands of a doctor who had offered his services.

Identification. It is our inescapable obligation to identify with others, to be present wherever elemental human need surfaces and calls out to us from deep places of hurt

CHAPTER 6

Loose Ends

They never quite got fitted into the over-all scheme. Leftovers, bits and pieces, sweepings, scattered thoughts— they have been accumulating for years in random style as the occasional commentary of one minister trying to stay in touch with the passing scene, outward and inward.

Most of these pieces were pastoral letters addressed to the ministers of churches in the metropolitan Boston area of the Massachusetts Conference, United Church of Christ, when I served as associate conference minister.

> We lack life's patience. . . . Life pursues her experiments far beyond the limitations of our judgment.
> —Dag Hammarskjöld

I was pulled up short by Peter Schrag's piece in the *New York Times,* "The Tunnel at the End of the Light." That phrase lights up the rough terrain we Americans inhabit these days. It means that the road to the future is not an uninterrupted, upward spiral. The long summer of wine and roses is drawing to a close. Chill winds, quite familiar to neighbors on the planet, have begun to penetrate the cracks and crannies of our snug insulation. The red carpet is being rolled up and stashed away. We are discovering what it's like to do business at the back door of history.

We have been inching toward the tunnel for quite a long time. How we manage the darkness that is likely to deepen will be a severe test: an economy in disarray; uncertainty in our international policies; mounting pressure upon those who are white, middle class, and well off by the poor and disinherited. Of course, if we recall only a little of our biblical heritage, none of this will surprise us. History has a Sovereign. The "Day of the Lord," said the prophet Amos, is, indeed, darkness and not light. "Why are the nations in turmoil? . . . The Lord who sits enthroned in heaven laughs them to scorn; then he rebukes them in anger [Psalm 2:4, NEB]."

Such brooding is appropriate for the days of Lent, the tunnel of the "church year," so to speak, with its gathering darkness and a cross looming in the shadows. There is a bleak segment in everyone's spiritual journey. If people of faith bypass it, they celebrate Easter prematurely, superficially; it is a false dawn heralded by tinny trumpets out of tune, with a colored egg for an offering.

Brothers and sisters, I am thinking of you in a special way at that time when being a minister is trickier and more spiritually exhausting than usual. And I crave for you a deeper understanding of Lent this year, not in spite of the hurts and hazards, but in the middle of them, and because of them. I crave it for you here in this narrowing of the way, in the paring away of excessive fat, in a sharper distinction between mere technique and solid substance, and, above all, in the bitter remembering, not of a crucifix, luminous with candlelight, but of the crucifixion of a young man all blood and unspeakable pain.

The crucifixion has never been a sign of defeat; it is the mark of faithfulness. And out of it, who can tell, we shall be able to shape something cleaner and braver and freer.

But hope, of course, implies a lot of patience, not giving up as soon as one of our ventures begins to show signs of failure.

As I understand it, Easter is all about that: that it comes light again, not because of any contriving on our part but because the God of all light wills it out of his incredible love for us, pressing in on us even in the darkest, loneliest stretches of the tunnel.

> By the grace of God I am what I am.
> —1 Corinthians 15:10

At a recent convocation of clergy, I was struck by the emphasis placed by that worthy body on ministers seeing themselves as "professionals." Unquestionably, professionalism is a matter to be kept in high visibility. Alongside it, but in no way antithetical to it, is the equally crucial business of paying attention to the person who is presumed to be at the core of the professional practitioner—a real, honest-to-God human being with his or her full share of lumps and liabilities, eccentricities, and rough edges, as well as a sizable capacity to be compassionate, long-suffering, and inspiring.

In one of his books, Samuel Miller recalls the unforgettable portrait of a minister named Dr. Jesperson drawn by Rainer Maria Rilke in *The Notebooks of Malte Laurids Brigge*. Being exceedingly pious by nature, the minister was entirely out of his element in any social situation. He was like a fish lying on dry ground, gasping. The trouble was that the only profession he had ever known was the soul. It was a public institution which he represented, and said Rilke, he saw to it that he was never off duty, not even in his relations with his wife.

Luckily, professional disasters, like Dr. Jesperson, are scarce among ministers. Our deviations from the norm of human authenticity are likely to take other, less blatant forms. The most common in my experience is a distorted understanding of faithfulness to duty, an "I-never-take-a-day-off" attitude.

In most instances, I do not question the integrity of

depth of commitment of such furiously busy and endlessly engaged people. But I do wonder sometimes if they recognize, as others probably do, how many "bubbles" have formed, how much their effectiveness as "professionals" has been eroded by their neglect of one aspect of authentic humanness, which is the capacity to be "off" the job as well as "on" it. At any rate, I have learned that it is the person behind professional accreditation who ultimately carries the responsibility for genuine spiritual communication.

Take it from one who has wrestled with the matter for years. I have a way to go, but I say to you from this point on my journey: take time, brother; take time, sister; take time to be *you!* Take time, now and then to be gaily, even cavalierly, aloof from the demands of your high calling. It releases all kinds of spiritual power. And people are looking for just that these days.

> They who wait for the Lord shall renew their strength.
> —Isaiah 40:31

Blow off the dust if you have to, but let me tell you an old story. It's about some Africans who were guiding a party of Americans on a long safari through the bush. The Americans had pushed the Africans hard for days, determined not to fall behind on their tight schedule. One morning, the guides went on strike, They refused to break camp. The Americans ordered, begged, and cajoled, but the Africans would not budge. All they would say was, "We have to stay here until our spirits catch up with our bodies."

It's where I am at the moment, here in early summer. Like you, I've been pushing hard most of the year. I need a stretch of open time. So the other day when a longer-than-usual breathing space came along, I sat on my back lawn for an hour. But something was missing. I realized that my spirit was somewhere back in early May!

It hasn't caught up with me yet, but it will, because God is good and because I intend to allow time for it to happen. I realize that a crisis can erupt, and like the bridesmaids in the Bible, I could be summoned at any moment by a midnight alarm. But short of that, I've dedicated time this summer to waiting.

With all the poise I can manage, I shall wait for weariness to drain away. I shall wait for events I may have misunderstood or mismanaged to fall into sharper focus and longer perspective. Without the hot breath of an agenda on my neck, I shall sit idly for a while, setting aside a few hours whose worth will be certified only to the degree that they are unproductive.

I shall wait for pain to ease, for joy to accumulate, to burst one day like a rocket over a darkened landscape, enabling me to celebrate the good things I have accomplished, especially the times when I have been able to turn people toward the light again. I shall wait for peace to fill empty, aching crevices; for knowledge, gained from the experience of the years, to season into wisdom.

It is a matter of waiting for the Spirit to return in its own good time, not according to my tightly planned schedule. There is something of the mystery and the might of the sea about it. The Spirit may come with the thundering explosion of a great breaker on a rocky headland. Or, it may come quietly, like the irrepressible force of the tide, inching across mud flats of disappointment and discouragement. But the Spirit comes—by the grace of God, it comes! And as Paul Tillich said once, "If we wait in hope and patience, the power of that for which we wait is already effective within us." In short, those who wait in patience have already received the power of that for which they wait.

I will covet for you this summer rest and renewal and the Spirit returning in power.

> The more faithfully you listen to the voice within you, the better you will hear what is sounding outside. And only he who listens can speak.
> —Dag Hammarskjöld

Some of you may remember that much of last year I was squared away against a manuscript deadline. I slugged my way finally to the last paragraph, packed the precious pages off, and, following an editorial conference, including an agreement to some changes, everything was cleared—"nihil obstat," "imprimatur." A late fall date was mentioned for publication.

I might have made it if I hadn't decided to read the whole thing through! I was elated at first, but gradually the sheen wore off. The going got harder, and along about the fourth chapter I ground to the nasty conclusion that it just wasn't right. None of it was downright bad; a lot of it made sense. I had something to say, and I had said it. But very little of it sang. In many places it simply droned. And where it should have danced, it limped.

Frustrated, I slammed the poor, aborted thing into a drawer, asked my editor to withdraw it from publication, and tried to forget it. But a stubborn demand for an accounting forced me to assess what had gone wrong.

I reached two conclusions, both of which, I am sure, delighted my Puritan conscience, which has always taken pleasure in my learning the lessons of adversity. The first was that what I had written was essentially dishonest. That is to say, while it was about my ideas, it wasn't about *me*, where I am now, the way I feel, rejoice, and hurt today. It ignored the surgery and scar tissue of recent years. It was antebellum. It bypassed one of the most stringent learnings of my interior warfare, namely, that what we have to say, if it is to be heard, must groan with our groans, ache with our own sharp pains, and laugh with our own unmistakable lilt.

The second conclusion was that I had *produced,* but I hadn't *created.* I had selected words, measured sentences into paragraphs, collected paragraphs into chapters, and met a deadline. In short, I had done little more than deliver a product for packaging.

It describes, I'm afraid, a lot of what I have been doing over the years: meeting the deadlines of a production schedule. And it's time to be done with it! What I need to know with certainty is that God is forever trying to get me out into the blowing of the fierce, unpredictable wind of the Spirit, roaring about the eaves of my snug retreats, rattling the locks of my shabby securities, trying to keep me faced into the wild gale of grace, until my eyes burn and my heart leaps up to take hold of "impossible possibilities."

> I remember *him*, his warm smile his salty approach, his enormous capacity for listening, his generous sharing of the treasure of his own experience.

I go back to the days of Fred Fagley, and that wasn't yesterday! Fred was one of the saints of the Congregational Christian dispensation in the 1930s and 1940s. I can't recall just what his official title was or what denominational agency he served. I do know that he spent a lot of his time in an itinerant ministry. He went up and down the land inviting ministers to talk with him about where they were, or weren't, in their calling, what their dreams where, where they were troubled.

I remember the morning I spent with him. I was serving a small, struggling church in metropolitan Chicago, two years out of seminary, still trying to find out which end was up. I'm hazy about any "process" he may have used to get me talking. All I know is that when he asked me to open up, I began to tell him freely what life in Oakton Church was like, how I felt about it, and where I wanted to go. I have forgotten now most of what he said, but what is important is that I remember *him*, his warm smile, his salty approach, his and loneliness, of abandonment and outrage. It is our obligation to say: "I hear you, I care, and I have come to stand with you for a little while, because, in one of the strange ways life is put together, your pain has become my pain, your need, my need."

Identification. My fellow ministers in the Lord, you know what it is about. You are identifying all the time with the sick and the bereaved, with the bewildered and the scared. It is the most difficult and treasured aspect of your ministry.

Identification. It is on my mind in a special way right now because of an experience of it I am having myself. As you know, some of us have been offering a presence, a standing by, during the days of carrying out the court order to desegregate the Boston public schools. My assignment at a school in Dorchester was a modest one. I was simply to be on hand, recognizable as a minister (I borrowed a clerical shirt and collar), and should the need arise, I was to do what I could to help cool passion and temper open hostility. As it turned out, thanks to the preparation of the principal and teachers, the good sense of parents, and the courage of the students, my services were not called upon. At first I had the sense of being useless, but when I talked with teachers and parents, I rediscovered the simple, uncomplicated strength of identification, of personal presence.

So, work at it all the time, counting it one of the strongest influences we wield in ministry. Identify with those who have been left out, for one reason or another, and speak out with gentle words as long as that is possible or with abrasive words, if necessary, in order that there be no mistaking where you stand.

> Comfort, comfort my people, says your God.
> —Isaiah 40:1

> When Ahab saw Elijah, Ahab said to him,
> "Is it you, you troubler of Israel?"
> —1 Kings 18:17

In a brilliant article, Richard Neuhaus pinpoints the situation of the contemporary church. It is described, he says, by the tension between *institution* and *mission*.

This, of course, is not a new insight. But the prevailing conditions under which the church exists these days bring it into sharp focus. We struggle to be faithful to our Lord, that is, to preach the gospel, to move onto new and exposed frontiers from time to time, and at the same time, we labor to survive as an institution, that is, to pay bills, to keep salary levels commensurate with a spiraling economy, and so on.

Institution involves the response to tradition; it is a solid anchorage in time and space. Mission involves the response to the prophetic, calling us to take risks in unexplored territory, bringing down fire from heaven. Christians live between these poles, and the quality of our life as a community of faith is tested by the tension we keep between them.

We are easily seduced by extremes. We may give in to the romanticism of those who would have little or nothing to do with the institutional, claiming that it is a major deterrent to authentic existence. But, as Neuhaus puts it, it is both theologically imperative and legitimate that we be concerned about the institution. It is simply another term for endurance. There is nothing in the structures of society that can endure without some form of institution.

On the one hand, we can surrender in a softheaded way to the notion that the present moment in society, or in the life of a congregation, is not an appropriate time for taking a prophetic, and probably abrasive, stance. Ministers can be heard saying that such was the role of the church in the 1960s but not in the 1970s. On the other hand, there are those who plead that they simply are not the "prophetic" type and are ill suited for making waves. The fact is, of course, that there is no exemption for any of us in such a matter. Whatever our personal style or particular gifts in ministry may be, there is no hiding place when the Word of God burns its way into the life of a congregation.

What I covet for us all, ministers and lay people, is a fresh awareness of the godly tension between *institution*, larded with and laced by tradition, and *mission*, exposed and vulnerable to the unpredictable winds of the Spirit. May you have such tension in your ministry and church, and with it the blessed knowledge when to tighten the tension, because the judgment of God demands it, and when to release it, because the reconciling spirit of Christ prompts it. So day by day, may you and your people live honorably at the ragged edges of faithfulness!

>   Christ climbed down
>   from His bare Tree
>   this year
>   and softly stole away into
>   some anonymous Mary's womb again
>   where in the darkest night
>   of everybody's anonymous soul
>   He awaits again
>   an unimaginable
>   an impossibly
>   Immaculate Reconception
>   the very craziest
>   of Second Comings.
>   —Lawrence Ferlinghetti*

---

*Lawrence Ferlinghetti, *A Coney Island of the Mind*. Copyright © 1958 by Lawrence Ferlinghetti. Reprinted by permission of New Directions Publishing Corporation.

Christmas could very well be that crazy this year! This year, especially: a shaky economy headed for some unknown collision with reality; a government in disarray; the voices of statesmen echoing in a moral vacuum; another eleventh-hour skirting of war; and an energy crisis growing worse all the time.

No one is wise enough to say where it will all lead, what changes are implied in American ways of living and doing business, or how uncomfortable and inconvenienced we shall be before we are through. It comes, eventually, to all sleek, fat societies like ours: the realization that we stand in tattered garments before an inevitable accounting of ourselves. We feel the chill of our near nakedness, and we are ashamed.

But praise God for seeds of hope in our midst! Praise also, however discomforting it may be, and for reasons known only to God, that we have been hammered together in such a way that we take the divine will most seriously at the borders of disaster, under the pressures of privation.

At any rate, it's the way I read the story behind the Story. It is the tale of a world subsisting at the edges of its own self-sufficiency, hurting enough, at long last, to be vulnerable to the only thing that can possibly rescue it—a love that comes into the cold and the dark to sit with all the crud and cruelty, to brood over it, to cradle it tenderly.

We know that it is in leanness rather than in fatness that we see and mark what things are important and what aren't. Moreover, in accepting the judgment that falls upon us, as well as upon corrupt public servants, we are better able to come to terms with our spiritual impoverishment. But greatest of all is the joy that is rooted in knowing that the intervention, the unmerited invasion of God's love, is into the clutter and confusion of anyone's ordinary, "anonymous soul!"

Christmas peace to you in all the deep places where it matters most!

> "Were you there when they crucified my Lord?
> Oh, sometimes it causes me to tremble."
> —Spiritual

Who was there the day Jesus was killed?

A lot of people were there.

The Pharisees were there—solid, law-abiding, respectable citizens, the "good people." But the young revolutionary from up-country terrified them. He ignored their rules, went about with riffraff, and was seen in disreputable places. He was too much of a threat to all the ways they knew of guaranteeing a stable society. He was too much for their sealed-up minds. So they made arrangements for his death. I was there, too. Any of us are there whenever Christ is crucified by blindness, bigotry, and sanctified, walled-in tradition.

Pontius Pilate and Caiaphas were there. All they were interested in was the scheme most likely to save their own skins. I was there. Any of us are there whenever Christ is crucified by expediency.

The mob was there, the mindless, fickle, emotion-swayed mob that shouted lusty hosannas on Sunday and then screamed obscenely for his death on Friday. I was there. Any of us is there whenever Christ is crucified by trying to hide in the crowd.

"Were you there when they crucified my Lord?" God knows it causes us to tremble, even to ask!

Trembling not so much at the agony, as at something else we see in the cross that catches us unaware and brings the tears: an understanding, an acceptance, a forgiveness that takes in even our cheapest denials, our most blatant betrayals. In the end, that's what Jesus' dying is about; it's what we mean when we say he died for us. It is to discover that in the face of extremity we are never left entirely to ourselves. The door of change is left open, and hopefully, some of us will walk through.

The apostle Paul said it best: "We are often troubled, but not crushed; sometimes in doubt, but never in despair; there are many enemies, but we are never without a friend; and though badly hurt at times, we are not destroyed."

I wish for you that strange kind of Easter victory.

> All things counter, original, spare, strange;
>   Whatever is fickle, freckled (who knows how?)
>   With swift, slow; sweet; sour; adazzle; dim;
> He father's-forth whose beauty is past change:
>   Praise him.
>   —Gerard Manley Hopkins

Being a reasonably ordered person, comfortable when things are well plotted in advance and trails are well marked, I am quite at home with the accent on *process*. I believe in each step coming in logical order, everything in sound psychological sequence from start to finish.

Nonetheless, I am uneasy at times over an undue emphasis on proper process at the expense of what I understand to be a distinguishing mark of the substance of our Christian faith. If I am right, there is a lot about it that is freewheeling, unpredictable, disorganized, a holy clutter of oddities, queer shapes, even queerer people, and light coming from the strangest places! Gerard Manley Hopkins talks about it in his poem "Pied Beauty."

> Glory be to God for dappled things. . . .
> All things counter original, spare, strange;
>   Whatever is fickle, freckled (who knows how?)[1]

From start to finish, the story is shot through with much that is out of line, ragged, on the grubby side, and not at all in keeping with a sophisticated modern perspective. There is the cow barn at the outset, a brash young rabbi shuttling from one obscure country town to another, and, at the end, an ignominious execution at the city dump.

You may call it a necessary tension between process and substance, to use precious contemporary jargon, but sometimes, I'm afraid, it is an obsessive need to be on the safe side. The alternative—and this is the risk that faith invites us to take—is simply letting something happen to us.

Essentially, Easter is something that *happened*. With all our human process and management skills we never could have designed that radiant, liberating event. It never would have occurred to us. But the blessed truth is that it *can* happen to us, and it is all the more likely if we'll allow it and quit our managing. It's creation all over again: whatever is counter and strange, fickle and freckled in our lives, is suddenly all ashine. It means a lot of waiting and much patience. It means expecting God to show up in the oddest places. It means that keeping the soil fertile is the primary condition for planning a garden.

> Whose records are we keeping?
> Whose script are we writing?
> Whose gains are we calculating?

You have had the experience more than once, I'm sure. It's part of the folkways of American churches. There is a film to be shown at a supper meeting. The lights go off. There is a whirring noise, a raucous blast of sound, a flicker of light on the screen, a dying moan on the speaker, and we're back to square one. The operator, an ever-willing volunteer technician, and the minister hover solicitously over the equipment. After a few minutes of winding and unwinding, screwing and unscrewing, tapping, jabbing, much muttering, and mild obscenity, recommended adjustments are made, and we're off. But, no go. A third attempt also fails. There is some desperate, last-minute tinkering, and we move onto the next item on the program.

When that happens, I confess to a perverse sense of satisfaction. It confirms my conviction that the fruits of our scientific, electronic knowhow are not wholly an unmixed blessing. I must admit, of course, and I realize that I am probably speaking for a small minority, that there are some of us who were never meant to cope with certain technological advances.

Widely recognized improvements escape us; their advantage over more familiar equipment eludes us. For example, I have a very old fashioned wristwatch with which I am perfectly content. I wind it in the morning, reset it to compensate for its unfailing two-minutes daily loss, and never give it another thought. It also has a little window that tells the day of the week and the date of the month; but since I never think of turning to a watch for that kind of data, I pay it no attention. (Nor have I ever been able to figure out how it works.)

The same holds for cameras. As far as I am concerned, the ultimate sophistication in photography was achieved in the Kodak Brownie that I had as a child. Zippers are often beyond me. Ditto for movie projectors, cassettes, and VCRs. I readily admit that this is merely an illustration of what has been called "a belated mind," commentary on my smug refusal to come to terms with the real world. Nonetheless, I submit a few questions for reflection.

With all the aids we have—visual, audio, stereophonic, electronic—we still need to ask: what commanding, overriding purpose are we aiding? We have typewriters that correct a mistake by the push of a button: whose script are we writing? We have computers with frightening capacities: whose records are we keeping? We have watches storing encyclopedic information (Victor Borge's uncle had one that told the time of twice-daily low tide in Hong Kong harbor): whose time are we keeping?

I have no allusions about it: "High tech" is here to stay.

There are unimaginable advances to be made. That's neither here nor there. What *is* here and very much at the center of things is an eternal Purpose that broods over all our cleverness, many of whose mysteries will never be uncovered. Before this sovereign intent for the world, we can only stand humble and in breathless awe, hoping that all our faces and our gadgets are set in the right direction!

> And after the fire
> A sound of gentle silence.
> —Davie Napier

Davie Napier's book *Word of God, Word of Earth* uncovers a treasure of truth-flashing gems. (This lyrical commentary on the story of Elijah bolsters one of my cherished notions, namely, that poets make the best biblical expositors and theologians.)

Take the scene where the dejected and self-pitying Elijah spends the night in a vast, echoing cave. It was, says Napier, his flight (like ours, at times) back to the womb, his craving for relief from coping with the uncopable. Suddenly, outside, there is chaos, first a tornado, then an earthquake, then a blistering fire. But, "not in the fire was Yahweh. And after the fire, a sound of gentle silence."

With a lifetime of conditioning by older translations where the words are "a still small voice," I had always assumed that what Elijah heard was the voice of God, and that the learning in this passage is to eschew violence and discord and know that God is apprehended only in quietness.

If I have his meaning straight, it wrenches me away from what has long been a comforting piece of spiritual wisdom. What he is pointing out is the sheer necessity, at times, for utter, stark silence; no soft murmurings in my ear, no gentle guarantee of relief from the ravaging of wind and fire and pain, but a stretch, long or short, of nothingness. Yet, it is a nothingness, a silence, that makes it possible for God to enter and to speak to us. We can be certain that the entrance will be at a time of God's own choosing and in God's own style; and the words we hear may not be entirely to our liking, as must have been so in the case of Elijah. For God said to him tersely, "Elijah, what on earth are you doing here, in a cave, with all that's yet to be done?"

No question about it, we'd never make it without a retreat to a cave now and then. But we also need this time for listening for "a sound of gentle silence," a time of preparation, a clearing away for the voice of Another. We can count on what we hear to be for our healing.

> "For the gate is narrow and the way is hard, that leads to life, and those who find it are few."
> —Matthew 7:14

A young man, twenty-nine, close and very dear to us in our family circle, has just died of cancer. He was a conscientious objector to war. He and his wife served in the Peace Corps. They were sharing their lives with their neighbors in a blighted, poverty-pocked section of Philadelphia. They found strength to hang on through the dark of impending death and of these days' sobering events in the loving, accepting community of a neighborhood Friends Meeting.

I joined a peace vigil on the Boston Common recently, and thought about Mark's life and his brave death. Mark was an interventionist, I decided. He inserted who he was, and particularly, his overriding commitment to peace, into the routine flow of people, opinions, and events. In his quiet, undemanding way, he required us to look into ourselves and to ponder what telling intervention each of *us* might possibly make into the same routine to arrest attention and pull the heart up short.

It was the same way with the nuns who were arrested the other day in St. Patrick's Cathedral in New York. Midway through the Mass, they prostrated their bodies in the aisle, symbols, they said, of the dead in Vietnam. Before the eyes of the cardinal, seated in ecclesiastical majesty on his throne, they were hauled away by the police on the grounds that they were impeding an act of Christian worship!

At such times, it is we, of course, who are blocked, immobilized, because we are so thoroughly habituated to church routine, "domesticated by its specious securities," to use Samuel Miller's words, frightened by deviations from the norm.

Mark and the nuns remind us, also, of the place of public demonstrations of conviction with their risky, life-laid-on-the-line dimension. Demonstrations can be upsetting; in a way, that's part of their function.

Recently they dedicated an addition to the Franklin Delano Roosevelt Library in Hyde Park in honor of Mrs. Roosevelt. In the middle of the stately ceremonies, a score of silent pickets appeared at the edge of the lawn holding signs protesting the expansion of a nearby Air Force Base. One of the men attending the service was heard to say, "Good, Eleanor would have approved!"

God gets things done in all kinds of ways, and, more often than not, it involves an individual bypassing the normal and the routine, with a personal intervention, bearing the price tag of private conscience.

"Attention, attention must be finally paid. . . ."
—Linda Loman in Arthur Miller, *Death of a Salesman*.

We've been living for quite a time now with the whole business of inclusive language. It's not going to go away, and we have a lot more work to do on it. It's no cinch, trying to get out from under the church's centuries-old patriarchal orientation. We keep saying "men," or "the brotherhood of man" when we really mean everybody. Or, we keep referring to God as "He" or "Him" without any regard to the fact that such language is deeply offensive to thousands of our fellow-members in the Church of Christ.

Maybe it isn't a problem for you; if it isn't, it should be! The issue is rooted in the deep emotions and convictions of women who share the journey of faith with men, and who are pressing hard for their full and unconditioned acceptance in the life of the church. And the language Christians use when we talk about them is a crucial aspect of the whole situation. The depth of their conviction, the hurt, and the humiliation they experience, in themselves, are reason enough for the rest of us to face the issue head-on. In Linda Loman's poignant words, "Attention, attention must finally be paid."

A few comments are in order. One is the necessity of a stepped-up vigilance over our vocabulary, refusing to be put off by those who dismiss the matter, saying that, after all, it's only a matter of words, and words can't be taken too seriously. It's quite the other way around, of course. The words we use are among the most powerful instruments we have, symbols of who we are and what we believe most passionately. Words and the ways we use them can be resonant with either blessedness or blasphemy.

Another point, we cannot weasel out on the subject by posting a notice to the effect that while we continue to use patently sexist language, we really don't mean to offend anybody. Moreover, will everyone please try to understand that we are speaking in a generic sense. Sorry, that won't play. It only compounds the offense.

Semantic traditionalists will have to accept the fact that inclusive language is not a passing fad. It is part and parcel of women's struggle toward liberation, and it can't be sidetracked. Moreover, it keeps slipping our minds that root-deep change is what the gospel is all about—making old things new.

One other consideration that I do not think can be easily dismissed: It is the effort to make whatever changes are called for in the name of liberation and inclusiveness as graceful as possible, avoiding language that is clumsy and ugly.

Let, the dialogue continue; and, sisters and brothers, watch your language!

NOTES

Foreword
1. John Newton, "Amazing Grace."

Chapter 1
1. Sallie TeSelle, *Literature and the Christian Life* (New Haven: Yale University Press, 1966), 76.
2. Dag Hammarskjöld, *Markings* (New York: Alfred A. Knopf, 1964), v.
3. Josephine Johnson, *Now in November* (New York: Simon & Schuster, 1935), 3.

Chapter 2
1. Eugene O'Neill, *The Iceman Cometh* (New York: Random House, Vintage Books, 1946), 116.
2. Tennessee Williams, *The Night of the Iguana* (New York: New Directions Books, 1962), 107.
3. Elia Kazan, *The Arrangement* (New York: Stein and Day, 1967), 422.
4. Barbara Tuchman, *The Guns of August* (New York: Dell Publishing Co., 1963), 485.

Chapter 3
1. Charles Péguy, *Péguy* (London: Dennis Hobson Ltd., 1946), 143.
2. Søren Kierkegaard, *Attack Upon Christendom* (Princeton, N.J.: Princeton University Press, 1944), 181.
3. Eugene O'Neill, *Long Day's Journey Into Night* (New Haven: Yale University Press, 1956), dedication.
4. Gerard Manley Hopkins, "God's Grandeur," in *Poems of Gerard Manley Hopkins*, 4th ed. (New York: Oxford University Press, 1967), 66.
5. Anne Sexton, "The Rowing Endeth," in *The Awful Rowing Toward God* (Boston: Houghton Mifflin Co., 1975), 85.

6. Frederick Buechner, *Telling the Truth* (New York: Harper & Row, 1977), 33.

Chapter 4
1. Henry David Thoreau, *Walden* (Boston: Houghton Mifflin Co., 1906), 350.
2. Rainer Maria Rilke, "Archaic Torso of Apollo," in *Selected Poems of Rainer Maria Rilke* (New York: Harper & Row Publishers, 1981), 47.
3. Marianne Moore, *Collected Poems* (New York: Macmillan Publishing Co., 1957), 40.
4. Tom Driver, *Poems of Doubt and Belief* (New York: Macmillan Co., 1964), 4, 5.
5. Randall Jarrell, "The Death of the Ball Turret Gunner," in *The Complete Poems* (New York: Farrar, Straus, and Giroux, 1969), 144.
6. Richard Wilbur, "Love Calls Us to the Things of This World," in *Things of This World* (San Diego, Calif.: Harcourt Brace Jovanovich, 1956), 5.
7. "Refreshment."
8. Marjorie Gibbons, "Tears."
9. Kevin E. Linagen, "Everything Dies in Winter."
10. Allan MacDougall, "Great Men and I."
11. Kim Albertson, "Gazing Into the Vast Expanse."
12. Albertson, "Civil Disobedience."
13. Margie Farmer, "More Than Once."
14. Gwendolyn Brooks, "Lovers of the Poor," in *Selected Poems* (New York: Harper & Row, Publishers, 1963), 90.
15. Wallace Stevens, "The Man With the Blue Guitar" in *Collected Poems of Wallace Stevens* (New York: Alfred A. Knopf, 1936), 165.
16. James Thurber, "The Seal Who Became Famous" in *The Thurber Carnival* (New York: Harper & Row Publishers, 1945), 257.
17. William Shakespeare, *Measure for Measure* in *The Riverside Shakespeare* (Boston: Houghton Mifflin Co., 1974).
18. Norman Cousins, *Anatomy of an Illness* (New York: W. W. Norton & Co., 1979), 29.
19. Peter DeVries, *The Blood of the Lamb* (Boston: Little, Brown, & Co., 1961), 237.
20. Shakespeare, *The Merchant of Venice,* Act V, Scene 1 in *The Riverside Shakespeare.*

21. Shakespeare, *The Life of Henry V,* Act IV, Prologue in *The Riverside Shakespeare.*
22. Shakespeare, Sonnet CXIV in *The Riverside Shakespeare,* 1770.
23. Robert Frost, *The Complete Poems of Robert Frost* (New York: Henry Holt & Co., 1967), 317.

Chapter 5
1. Frederick Buechner, *Telling the Truth* (New York: Harper & Row Publishers, 1977), 36, 35.
2. Dylan Thomas, *The Poems of Dylan Thomas* (1939), reprinted in *Norton Anthology of Modern Poetry* (New York: W.W. Norton, 1973), 911.

Chapter 6
1. Gerard Manley Hopkins, "Pied Beauty" in *Poems of Gerard Manley Hopkins,* 4th ed. (New York: Oxford University Press, 1967), 69.